Mary's baby, Jesus, was born in a stable in Bethlehem.

[See page 13

THE BIBLE

IN PICTURES

EDITED BY

THE REV. RALPH KIRBY

EDITORIAL CONSULTANTS

THE REV. PROFESSOR E. O. JAMES, M.A., D.Litt., Ph.D., D.D., F.S.A.

THE REV. C. C. MARTINDALE, M.A.

PROFESSOR S. H. HOOKE, M.A., D.D., F.S.A.

GREYSTONE PRESS

NEW YORK

Preface

THIS is a Bible Picture Book—with a difference. There are over a thousand illustrations with a simple text based on the Authorized Version, so designed that the Bible lives. The pictures are packed with action, and flow into one another in such a manner that the movement of the story is clearly seen. The whole is so presented that children as well as adults may see and understand.

Christian civilization draws its inspiration from the eternal purpose of God revealed in the Bible, and in particular in its central figure, Jesus Christ. But the Bible is a difficult book for the average person to read, and for three reasons: (1) We have been taught to take up a book and read it straight through, beginning at the first page and continuing to the last. The Bible does not lend itself easily to that method; it is a library rather than one book. (2) Our language has changed considerably since the Authorized Version—still the most popular—was written, and even in American translations there are expressions with which our eye and ear are unfamiliar. (3) More and more we are being accustomed to see, and less and less are we able easily to grasp lengthy or involved and complicated reading.

So in this book we have selected the main stories of the Bible, and used the pages as a screen on which to project their movement; keeping, in the briefest possible captions, the essential parts of the story in language based on the Authorized Version but tuned to our modern ear. There are three sections: "The Story of Jesus"; its background, "The Story of His People"; and its sequel, "The Story of His Church."

The Bible belongs to all Christians. Though this book has been designed, written and produced by a Methodist, editorial consultants of other faiths have been unremitting in their counsel and assistance. The editor wishes to express his most sincere indebtedness to them for their zeal and watchfulness. Every care has been taken to make this book both accurate and memorable in its presentation. If there should be anything in it which causes any reader or "viewer" misgivings, it must be placed to the account of the editor himself!

We are indebted to the artists for the skill with which they have interpreted the editor's suggestions, and the devotion and reverence with which they have undertaken their most difficult and delicate task.

I pray that this book may bring a fresh vision of Christ, and God's purpose in Him, to you who now read it in the midst of the heartache and frustration of our modern world.

RALPH KIRBY

CONTENTS

PART I

THE STORY OF JESUS

Page 9

6

PART II
THE STORY OF HIS PEOPLE

PART III
THE STORY OF HIS CHURCH

COLOR ILLUSTRATIONS BY HARRY COLLER AND KENNETH INNS
BLACK AND WHITE ILLUSTRATIONS BY ELSIE WALKER, DOUGLAS RELF,
DESMOND WALDUCK, E. WALLCOUSINS, M. MACKINLAY, C. S. GOULD,
MARJORIE WHITTINGTON, A. W. LACEY, SELBY DONNISON

PART I

The Story of Jesus

IN these pages you will see unfold before your eyes the greatest
drama of all time. It is based upon the Gospels of Matthew,
Mark, Luke and John—the first four books of the New Testament.
Like countless numbers of men, women, and children before you,
you will find it brings you courage and comfort, and lifts up your
heart.

Here you will journey in strange and distant lands and be an eye-
witness to marvelous happenings. With the wise men of the East you
will follow a star to Bethlehem. You will watch the wondrous Child
grow to wondrous Manhood. You will walk with Him and talk with
Him, behold His kindly deeds of healing and consolation, and hear
His message by the lake, on the hillside and in the city street. You
will learn eternal truths about God and the life of man that will
inspire and thrill you.

With the disciples you will sit in the Upper Room and partake of
the Last Supper. You will climb up the Mount of Olives and tarry
in a garden called Gethsemane. You will stand amid the jostling
Roman soldiery while Pilate judges in his palace, and you will walk
the long way to Calvary. But in the garden of the empty tomb you
will meet Him again, and on the mountain in Galilee, and there He
will promise to be with you always.

The birth
of a
prophet

1. In the days when Herod the Great was king over Judea——

2. —there lived there a priest, named Zacharias, and his wife, Elisabeth, a God-fearing couple, who were already growing old and had no children.

3. But the angel Gabriel came to the priest in the Temple at Jerusalem, and promised that they should have a son. "You must call him John," said the angel.

4. "How can I be sure of this?" cried Zacharias. "My wife and I are too old to have children!" Gabriel replied: "As a sign, you shall be struck dumb until the child is born and named." And when Zacharias reappeared before the people, he could not speak.

10

5. Elisabeth did have a baby and her friends and relations, when they heard, rejoiced with her. When it came to the naming of the child, however——

6. —they wished to call him Zacharias. "No," said Elisabeth, "he shall be called John." "But none of your family has this name," they protested.

7. Then they made signs to Zacharias to discover what name he wished to give the child. He wrote on his writing tablet: "His name is John."

8. And while they all marvelled, Zacharias found he was able to speak again, and he at once began to praise God.

9. John lived in the desert, to fit himself to fulfil Gabriel's prophecy: "He shall make ready a people prepared for the Lord."

Tidings for Mary

1. Gabriel also came to Mary, a young woman about to marry Joseph of Nazareth.

2. He greeted her and said: "You will bear a son and call Him Jesus. The Holy Spirit will come upon you and therefore the holy child shall be called the Son of God."

3. Mary bowed her head and answered: "I am the servant of God." And when Gabriel had gone she visited Elisabeth, who hailed her as the future mother of the Lord.

4. Then Mary sang these words, which we call *The Magnificat:*

My soul doth magnify the Lord, and my spirit hath rejoiced in God my Saviour.

For He hath regarded the lowliness of His handmaiden: for behold, from henceforth all generations shall call me blessed.

For He that is mighty hath magnified me and holy is His name.

And His mercy is on them that fear Him throughout all generations.

He hath showed strength with His arm; He hath scattered the proud in the imagination of their hearts.

He hath put down the mighty from their seats, and exalted the humble and meek.

He hath filled the hungry with good things; and the rich He hath sent empty away.

He, remembering His mercy, hath holpen His servant Israel, as he promised to our forefathers, to Abraham, and his seed for ever.

5. Some months later, after Joseph had married Mary, they saw posted in Nazareth the proclamation of a census decreed by the Roman Emperor, Augustus.

6. This meant that every man had to go to the city where he was born to record the names of his family for taxing. As Joseph was of the House of David he and Mary travelled from Nazareth, in Galilee, to Bethlehem, which was David's city in Judea. It was nearly time for Mary's Child to be born.

7. When they reached Bethlehem, the city was so crowded that there was no room for them at the inn except in the stable. There Mary's baby, Jesus, the Son of God was born, and she wrapped Him in swaddling clothes and laid Him in a manger.

The shepherds hear the news

1. Now in the country near Bethlehem there were shepherds who were watching over their flocks by night.

2. Suddenly an angel appeared and said: "I bring you good tidings of great joy which shall be to all people. For there is born this day in the city of David a Saviour, which is Christ the Lord. And this shall be a sign unto you.

3. "You shall find the Babe wrapped in swaddling clothes, lying in a manger." Suddenly the heavens were full of angels saying: "Glory to God in the highest, and on earth peace, goodwill toward men."

4. The shepherds said to one another, "Let us go to Bethlehem." And they ran to the stable and found Mary and Joseph and the baby Jesus.

5. When they had seen Him they told everyone what the angel had said to them concerning Him; and all who heard them were amazed. Then the shepherds returned, praising God for all the things they had seen.

15

The wise men seek the child

1. When Jesus was born, wise men in the East saw a brilliant star shining, which they were sure meant that the Jewish Messiah had come. So they went to Herod's court.

2. They asked the king where the Child was who was born King of the Jews, for they wished to worship Him. Herod, after questioning his chief priests, sent them to Bethlehem, saying: "When you have found Him, bring me word so that I may come and worship Him also."

16

"Lord, save me!" Peter cried when he began to sink.

[See page 63

"Who do you say I am?" "Thou art the Christ, the Son of the Living God!"

[*See page* 66

The children were there, too, crying: "Hosanna in the highest!"

[*See page* 112

"Thou knowest I have power to crucify Thee?" said Pilate.

[*See page* 144

"I am with you always, even unto the end of the world."

[*See page* 159

Moses was found on the river's bank by Pharaoh's daughter.

[*See page* 181

David took a stone and slung it straight at Goliath, the Philistine.

[See page 203

Saul said: "Who art Thou, Lord?" And the Lord said: "I am Jesus."

[*See page* 270

3. Then the wise men mounted their camels and set off to Bethlehem; and the star which they had seen in the East went before them till it stood over where the young Child was.

4. And when they came into the house they saw the Child Jesus with Mary, His mother, and bowed down and worshipped Him. When they had opened their treasures they presented to Him the royal gifts they had brought with them—gold, frankincense and myrrh.

5. But they did not return to King Herod's court. For that night, as they lay sleeping, an angel, sent from God, appeared to them in a dream, warning them. So they left Bethlehem and returned to their own country by another way.

17

The flight into Egypt

1. Joseph also fled with Mary and the baby Jesus, for God's angel had appeared to him as well, warning him that Herod, being jealous, intended to destroy the young Child. "Seek safety in Egypt," said the angel, "and remain there until I bring you word."

2. When he realized he had been tricked Herod was furious, for he feared that the Child born King of the Jews would threaten his own throne. So he ordered that all children of two years old and under in Bethlehem and the surrounding district should be killed.

3. So the children were put to death, and everywhere was heard the sound of their parents' weeping.

4. Not until the angel had told them that it was safe to return to Palestine did Joseph, Mary and Jesus leave Egypt.

5. Joseph decided that they should return home to Nazareth, which was in Galilee, for although he had now learned King Herod was dead, Joseph knew that Archelaus, Herod's son, ruled in Judea, and feared lest he, too, should seek to destroy the Child.

6. There Joseph plied his trade as a carpenter, and taught Jesus, who became known as the "Son of the carpenter." Jesus grew into boyhood beloved by all, and God's grace was reflected in everything He said and did.

Jesus and the Rabbis

1. Every year Joseph and Mary journeyed to Jerusalem——

2. —for the Feast of the Passover. When Jesus was twelve years old He went with His parents to celebrate the Feast, in which the Jews commemorate God's deliverance of Israel from the Egyptians and the founding of their nation.

3. On the way home to Nazareth, however, Joseph and Mary missed Jesus at the end of the first day's march. They sought Him in the tents of their friends and relatives but could not find Him. So they had to go back to Jerusalem to look for Him.

4. And there they found Him in the Temple, sitting among the learned teachers of religion, both hearing them and asking them questions. And all those who heard Him were astonished at His understanding and His answers.

5. Mary reproached Him: "Why have you done this to us? Your father and I have sought you, sorrowing." Jesus said gently: "Did you not know that I must be about My Father's business?" They did not understand that He spoke of God's work.

6. Then they returned to Nazareth. Until He was nearly thirty years old, Jesus, our Saviour, lived and worked as the carpenter's son, learning Joseph's trade and growing in wisdom and stature and in favor with God and man.

The baptism of Jesus

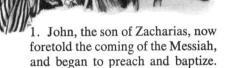

1. John, the son of Zacharias, now foretold the coming of the Messiah, and began to preach and baptize.

2. Jesus Himself, who was about thirty years old, made the journey from Nazareth to be baptized by John in the River Jordan.

3. When John saw Jesus coming, he said: "Dost Thou come to me, when I have need to be baptized by Thee?"

4. But Jesus persuaded John to baptize Him. Immediately afterwards the heavens were opened; the Spirit of God descended like a dove alighting on Him, and a voice from heaven said: "This is my beloved Son in Whom I am well pleased."

23

The temptation of Jesus

1. Jesus was now tested. For forty days and nights He was alone in the wilderness save for the wild beasts. During that time He ate nothing, and when it ended He was hungry.

2. The devil tempted Him: "If Thou be the Son of God, command that these stones be made bread." But Jesus would not.

3. He answered: "It is written in the Scriptures, 'Man shall not live by bread alone but by every word that proceeds out of the mouth of God.' "

4. Then Jesus was tempted to cast Himself from a high tower of the Temple at Jerusalem. "If Thou be God's Son, angels shall bear Thee up," said the tempter.

5. "Thou shalt not tempt the Lord thy God," replied Jesus. So the devil took Him to a high mountain, showed Him all the kingdoms of the world and the glory of them, in a moment of time, and said: "All these will I give Thee if Thou wilt fall down and worship me."

6. But Jesus turned and answered the devil sternly: "Get thee hence, Satan, for it is written in the Scriptures, 'Thou shalt worship the Lord thy God and Him only shalt thou serve.'" When the devil saw that Jesus was firm against temptation, he left Him. Then angels came and ministered to Him.

Jesus calls his first disciples

1. The first followers of Jesus came to Him in this way.

2. John the Baptist one day turned to two of his followers, who were fishermen (Andrew and John), as Jesus walked by, and said: "Behold the Lamb of God!"

3. The two men at once followed Jesus and spoke to Him, and He invited them to come to the house where He was staying. But Andrew first went to his brother, Simon,

26

4. The next day Jesus chose Philip, from Bethsaida, and said to him: "Follow me."

5. Philip said to Nathanael: "We have found the Messiah in Jesus of Nazareth."

6. But Nathanael scornfully answered: "Can any good thing come out of Nazareth?" Philip, in reply, led him to Jesus.

saying: "We have found the Messiah!" Andrew brought Simon to Jesus, and when Jesus saw him He said: "Simon, you shall be called 'Peter' "—meaning "a rock."

7. But when Jesus told him that He had known and seen him under the fig-tree before Philip called him, Nathanael said: "Master, You are the Son of God."

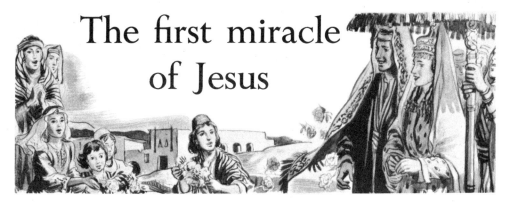

The first miracle of Jesus

1. Three days later there was a wedding in the town of Cana, in Galilee, and among the guests invited were Mary, the mother of Jesus, and Jesus Himself and His disciples.

2. During the feast Mary came to Jesus troubled: "The guests have no wine!" she said, and looked at Him. "Mine hour has not yet come——" He began.

3. But Mary turned to the servants, "Whatever He tells you, do!" "Then fill these water-pots with water," said Jesus; and they filled them to the brim.

4. When Jesus commanded them to pour the water, they found it was wine. They took it to the guests, and the governor of the feast praised the bridegroom for its quality. Only the servants who had drawn the water knew the secret. This was the first of the miracles.

Nicodemus

1. On one occasion when Jesus went to Jerusalem for the Feast of the Passover, Nicodemus, one of the chief Pharisees, visited him by night. He acknowledged Jesus as a teacher come from God, but could not understand all He taught.

2. For Jesus said: "A man must be born again if he is to see the Kingdom of God." "How can this be?" Nicodemus asked. Jesus answered: "He must be 'born again' by water and the Spirit—his rebirth is not of the body but spiritual."

29

The woman
by the well

1. On the way back to Galilee Jesus went through Samaria. At Sychar He rested by the well while His disciples went to buy food.

2. A woman came to draw water. When Jesus asked her for a drink she was startled, for Jews had no dealings with Samaritans.

3. When He told her of her past life, she knew that He was a prophet, and Jesus confessed to her that He was the Messiah.

4. The woman left her water-pot, ran to the city, and told the townsfolk that she had found the Messiah. So the people left the city and went out to Him.

5. Many at once believed in Him and begged Him to stay. For two days He taught them; then they said: "This is truly the Christ, the Saviour of the world!"

The nobleman's son

1. On leaving Sychar, Jesus returned to Cana, there to be joyfully greeted by the Galileans who had been at Jerusalem at the time of the feast and seen what He had done there.

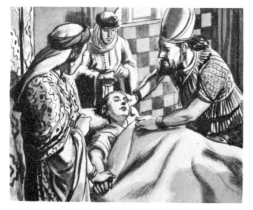

2. A nobleman who had a son lying ill at Capernaum came to beg Jesus to heal the boy for it was feared that he would die.

3. "Go your way," said Jesus, "for your son will live." And believing the word of Jesus the nobleman obeyed Him and went.

4. As he drew near to Capernaum, his servants came to meet him, saying: "Your son is alive!" He asked them at what time the boy had begun to recover.

5. They said: "Yesterday, at one o'clock." Then he remembered that that was the exact hour at which Jesus had told him that his son would live.

31

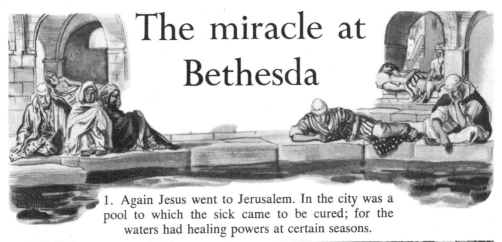

The miracle at Bethesda

1. Again Jesus went to Jerusalem. In the city was a pool to which the sick came to be cured; for the waters had healing powers at certain seasons.

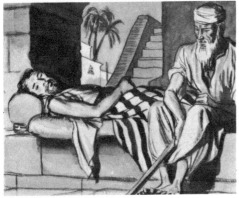

2. Among those lying by the pool, which was called Bethesda, was a man who had been ill for thirty-eight years. Jesus, knowing of his plight, said to him:

3. "Do you really want to be made well?" "No one will help me into the pool," he replied. "Rise, take up your bed and walk!" commanded Jesus.

4. And the man was healed at once, and rose and took up his bed; but the priests rebuked him for carrying it on the Sabbath.

5. "I was told to do so," he replied. He did not know Jesus' name, but later, in the Temple, pointed Him out to the priests.

Nazareth rejects Jesus

1. When John the Baptist was imprisoned for denouncing Herod Antipas' marriage to his brother's wife——

2. —Jesus returned to Galilee, healing the sick and preaching everywhere: "The Kingdom of God is at hand." One Sabbath at Nazareth He claimed for Himself the prophecy of Isaiah: "The Spirit of the Lord is upon Me because He has anointed Me to preach, to heal and to set at liberty."

3. At this the congregation angrily drove Him from the synagogue, for to the people of Nazareth Jesus was simply the son of Joseph the carpenter, and had no right to claim to be the Lord's anointed. "In his own country," said Jesus, "a prophet has no honor."

4. So angry were the crowds that they thrust Him right out of the town and led Him to the brow of the hill on which Nazareth was built, intending to throw Him down headlong. But He passed calmly through the midst of them, and went His way unscathed.

"Fishers of men"

1. One day at Capernaum Jesus saw Andrew and Peter cleaning their nets.

2. Jesus taught the crowds on the shore from Peter's boat. Afterwards He told Peter to launch out into the deep and let down his nets.

3. "We have fished all night and caught nothing," said Peter, "but we will obey." When they did so, there were so many fish that their nets broke.

4. And Peter and all with him—for he had called James and John to help bring in the fish—were astonished. Jesus said: "Fear not! Follow Me and I will make you fishers of men." And when they had brought their boats to land they left everything and followed Him.

The divine healer

1. On the Sabbath Jesus taught in the synagogue at Capernaum, amazing all with His knowledge.

2. During the service a man who had fits of madness suddenly shrieked: "I know who Thou art—the Holy One of God!" Jesus rebuked the spirit of madness, saying: "Silence! Come out of him." The man, after falling in a fit, recovered, and was calm again, his mind healed.

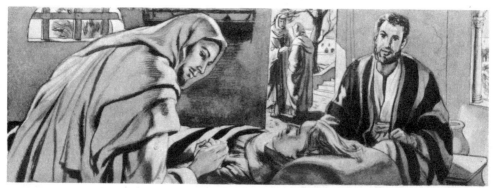

3. When they left the synagogue, Jesus and His disciples went home to Peter's house; and when Jesus heard that the mother of Peter's wife was ill with a serious fever, He took her by the hand, and immediately the fever left her.

4. In the evening, when the sun set, the crowds brought to Him all those people who were sick and suffering in mind and in body, beseeching Him to cure them; for His fame had already spread. Then Jesus laid His hands on the diseased and healed them.

The sermon
on the mount

Seeing the crowds, Jesus went up into a mountain and taught them saying:

"Blessed are the poor in spirit: for theirs is the kingdom of heaven.

"Blessed are they that mourn: for they shall be comforted.

"Blessed are the meek: for they shall inherit the earth.

"Blessed are they which do hunger and thirst after righteousness:
for they shall be filled.

"Blessed are the merciful: for they shall obtain mercy.

"Blessed are the pure in heart: for they shall see God.

"Blessed are the peacemakers: for they shall be called the children of God.

"Blessed are they which are persecuted for righteousness' sake:

for theirs is the kingdom of heaven.

"Blessed are ye, when men shall revile you and persecute you, and shall say all manner of

evil against you falsely for My sake.

"Rejoice, and be exceeding glad:

for great is your reward in heaven: for so persecuted they

the prophets which were before you.

"And after this manner you should pray:

"Our Father which art in heaven,

Hallowed be Thy name.

"Thy kingdom come.

Thy will be done in earth as it is in heaven.

"Give us this day our daily bread.

"And forgive us our trespasses, as we forgive them that trespass against us.

"And lead us not into temptation, but deliver us from evil;

For Thine is the kingdom, and the power, and the glory, for ever and ever. Amen."

Jesus heals a leper

1. As Jesus was praying in a solitary place, the disciples came, saying: "All men seek Thee!"

2. So Jesus went with them, preaching and healing throughout Galilee. Crowds of people followed Him wherever He travelled.

3. While Jesus taught there came a leper kneeling before Him and saying: "If Thou wilt, Thou canst make me clean!"

4. Jesus was deeply moved. He put out His hand and touched him, saying: "I will; be clean!" Immediately the leper was cured.

5. And the man was so full of joy that, in spite of Jesus' warning that he should tell no one of his cure, he told everyone.

A cripple and his friends

1. Jesus returned to Capernaum, and among the crowds thronging round the house were four men who had brought their paralyzed friend to be healed. As they could not get through the crowd, they took him up to the flat roof, tore a hole in it and let him down at Jesus' feet.

2. Jesus said to the sick man: "Son, your sins are forgiven." But He knew the scribes thought His words were blasphemous——

3. —for God alone could forgive sins. So, to prove His authority, Jesus healed him, saying: "Take up your bed, and go home."

The disciple Matthew

1. Among the tax-collectors for the Romans at Capernaum was one called Matthew.

2. Jesus saw Matthew and said to him: "Follow Me." Matthew at once obeyed. That evening he asked Jesus to a feast.

3. Jesus ate with Matthew's friends, including many tax-gatherers, who were despised because they worked for the Romans.

4. Then the Pharisees came to His disciples and questioned them: "Why do you and your Master eat and drink with tax-gatherers and sinners?"

5. When Jesus heard He said: "Those who are well need no doctor, but those who are ill. I have come not to call the righteous but sinners to repentance."

The true religion

1. When the Pharisees saw Jesus and His disciples plucking and eating corn as they walked in the fields on the Sabbath, they objected, for they considered this unlawful on the holy day.

2. Jesus said: "The Sabbath was made for man, and not man for the Sabbath." Later the same day in the synagogue Jesus saw a man with a withered hand. The Pharisees watched to see whether He would heal him. Jesus called the man, and then asked the Pharisees:

3. "Is it lawful to do good on the Sabbath?" They would not answer. Jesus told the man to stretch out his hand and it was seen to be completely healed.

4. The angry Pharisees went at once to plot Jesus' death with the Herodians. So the religious and political parties joined forces against Him.

Jesus chooses His twelve apostles

1. Jesus, knowing that the Pharisees and Herodians were plotting to kill Him, now took steps to make sure that His work was carried on when He had gone from the earth. So He called to Him His disciples, and of them He chose twelve whom He called apostles, or men "sent out as messengers." Their names were: Simon (who was now known as Peter), and Andrew his brother; James and John, the sons of Zebedee; Philip and Bartholomew; Matthew, the tax-collector, and Thomas; James, the son of Alpheus, and Lebbeus Thaddeus; Simon the Zealot, a Canaanite; and Judas Iscariot, who betrayed Jesus.

JAMES
THE LESS

SIMON
THE
ZEALOT

JOHN

JUDAS

THADDEUS

2. These twelve Jesus sent first as missionaries to the Jews. "Go," He said, "to the lost sheep of the House of Israel, and preach, saying, 'The Kingdom of Heaven is at hand!' Heal the sick, cleanse the lepers, raise the dead, cast out devils." He added that they need take with them neither money, food nor clothes, for the people they visited would provide for them. They were to bless those who treated them kindly, but to abandon any town that would not receive them. Then Jesus warned His disciples that they would often have to suffer for His sake, but comforted them with: "He who loses his life for My sake shall find it."

A Roman's faith

1. In Capernaum a Roman army officer, whose servant lay ill and near to death, heard that Jesus had returned to the town.

2. He asked the elders of the synagogue to beg Jesus to heal his servant. They at once told Jesus how deserving the officer was of help, for he had built them a synagogue. As Jesus and the elders neared the centurion's house, friends brought this message from him:

3. "Lord, I am not worthy enough for you to enter my house; only say the word and my servant shall be healed." Jesus marvelled at his faith, greater than any He had found in Israel.

4. And He sent this reply: "As you have believed so shall it be done!" And the servant was healed as He had promised.

The widow's son

1. Next day Jesus visited Nain. Near the city gates He saw the body of a young man carried out on a stretcher.

2. The dead man was the only son of a widow. Our Lord was deeply moved for her, and comforted her: "Do not weep."

3. Then He touched the stretcher. Those carrying it stood still, and Jesus said: "Young man: I say unto you, arise."

4. At once, to the astonishment and fear of all, the dead man sat up and began to speak, and Jesus brought him to his mother. Everyone praised God; some said that a great prophet had arisen among them, and others that God Himself had come among His people, and this report of Him spread throughout Judea.

Jesus rebukes a Pharisee

1. A certain Pharisee, named Simon, asked Jesus to eat with him at his house, so Jesus went with him.

2. While they sat eating, a woman, who was known to be a sinner, came into Simon's house. In her hands she bore an alabaster box of ointment. She stood behind Jesus, weeping; the tears fell fast over His feet and she wiped them away with her hair.

3. When Simon saw that Jesus allowed her to kiss His feet and anoint them he thought: "This Man, if He were really a prophet, would have known the sort of woman this is who touches Him, for she is a sinner." Then Jesus turned to Simon. "Simon," He began, "I have something to say to you." Simon replied: "Say on, Master." "Two men owed money to a certain man," Jesus continued. "One owed him a very large sum and the other merely the tenth part of that sum. When he saw they could not pay, he freely forgave them both. Tell me, which of them would love him most?" "I suppose the one to whom he forgave most," Simon replied. "Yes," said Jesus. He added: "This woman has done all you failed to do to make Me welcome—she has washed My feet, and anointed them, and kissed them without ceasing—and so, although her sins are many, they are all forgiven because her love is great."

4. Jesus turned back to the woman and repeated His words: "Your sins are forgiven. Your faith has saved you—go in peace." But those of Simon's friends who had been sitting eating with Him began to ask themselves: "Who is this that forgives even sins?"

49

He cures a dumb man

1. One day there was brought to Jesus a man who was blind and dumb. The Jews believed that such a man was possessed of a devil, for they thought that disease was caused by sinfulness.

2. When, therefore, Jesus cured the man, although the people said He must be the Messiah, the Pharisees said that His power to cast out devils came from the Prince of Devils himself. Jesus answered: "Would Satan cast out Satan?

3. "If he did," Jesus continued, "he would be fighting against himself. But if I cast out devils by the Spirit of God then the Kingdom of God is come to you. He that is not with Me is against Me: beware, therefore, lest you blaspheme against the Holy Spirit of God."

His true family

1. When His family heard that the teachings of Jesus had set the religious and political powers against Him and that plots were being made to kill Him, they said: "He is mad!" and came to bring Him home.

2. But the people were so crowded about the house that His family could not get through and had to send word to Him.

3. The people who sat around Jesus, listening to Him, said: "Your mother and your brethren are outside asking for you."

4. But Jesus answered them by saying: "Who is my mother? Who are my brethren?" Then He stretched out His hands towards His disciples and said: "Here are my mother and brethren! Whoever does God's will is my brother and my sister and my mother."

The parable of the sower

1. The same day Jesus, from a boat on the lake, told the crowds on the shore of His work, comparing His word to seed and the fate of His teaching to its fate.

2. "A sower went forth to sow," said Jesus, "and some of his seed fell by the wayside. At once the birds flew down and ate it up.

3. "Some fell on rocky ground and died for lack of soil.

4. "Some fell among thorns and was choked by them.

5. "But some fell on good ground and yielded fine wheat, some thirty, some sixty and some a hundred times as much."

52

The parable of the tares

1. At the same time Jesus told other parables to explain the nature of the Kingdom of Heaven.

2. One of His stories was this: "The Kingdom of God," said Jesus, "is like a man who sowed good seed in his field.

3. "But his enemy came while his men slept and sowed weeds among the wheat. When the grain began to grow, so did the weeds.

4. "'An enemy did this!' said the master, but would not let his men pull up the weeds lest the wheat was pulled up too.

5. "'At harvest-time,' he said, 'the reapers will gather the weeds and burn them, but the wheat will be gathered into my barn.'"

53

"The Kingdom of Heaven"

1. More and more the people came to Jesus as He was by the seaside to hear Him preach, and He taught them what the Kingdom of Heaven was like by telling them simple stories.

2. "It is like hidden treasure which is suddenly uncovered by a man at the plough; full of joy he hides it until he has sold all he has to buy the field for himself.

3. "Or imagine a merchant seeking the finest pearls. One day he finds the richest pearl he has ever seen, so he sells all his other pearls to buy it.

4. "The Kingdom of Heaven is like a little bit of yeast which a woman puts in three measures of flour. It leavens the whole.

5. "Yet again, it is like a fishing-net thrown into the sea, and when it is full the good is kept, but the bad is cast away!"

A storm at sea

1. In the evening Jesus bade farewell to the crowds and embarked for the other side with His disciples.

2. Suddenly a great storm-wind blew up, and the waves beat into the ship so that it was full of water and in danger of sinking. The terrified disciples woke Jesus, who lay asleep on a pillow in the stern of the ship, crying: "Lord, save us, we perish!"

3. Then Jesus rose up and rebuked the wind, and cried to the waves: "Peace! Be still!" The wind ceased and there was a great calm. Turning to His disciples He said: "Why are you so full of fear? Where is your faith?" But they in fear murmured to each other: "What kind of a Man is this? Even the wind and the sea obey Him."

The madman among the tombs

1. As they drew near the shores of Gadara, a madman, who had long lived among the tombs, ran to meet them.

2. He cried to Jesus as He stepped ashore: "Torment me not!" "What is your name?" Jesus asked. "Legion! For there are many devils in me!"

3. Jesus said: "Go!" and the madness left the man. At that moment a herd of swine feeding nearby ran down the hill into the sea as if the devils had entered them!

4. The herdsmen fled in terror to the city, and told the news. All the people came out and saw the madman with Jesus, clothed and quite sane again.

5. But they were afraid and asked Jesus to go. The man wished to follow Him, but Jesus said: "Go home to your friends and tell them what God has done to you."

57

The daughter of Jairus

1. On His return Jesus was approached by Jairus, a ruler of the synagogue, whose daughter was close to death. "Come and lay your hands on her," he begged, "and she will live."

2. As Jesus went with Jairus the crowds pressed round Him, and one woman, who had spent all she had on doctors without being cured, came behind and touched the edge of His robe; "For," she said, "if I but touch His garment I shall be well."

3. Jesus turned at once, saying: "Who touched Me?" The woman, trembling, confessed. "Daughter, your faith has healed you," said Jesus. "Go in peace."

4. At that moment a messenger came to tell Jairus that his child had died. But Jesus turned to Jairus. "Do not fear," He said. "Only believe."

5. When they came to the house Jesus dismissed the hired mourners, saying: "Why do you weep and wail? The girl is not dead: she is asleep." But they laughed at Him scornfully.

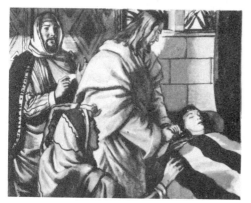

6. As soon as they had gone, Jesus took the girl's parents and three of His disciples into the room with Him.

7. He took the girl by the hand and said: "Get up, my child!" Her life was restored, and she opened her eyes.

8. And immediately the girl, who was twelve years old, got up and walked, to the astonishment of all. Then Jesus told her mother and father to give her something to eat and commanded that no one should be told of the miracle. Nevertheless, reports of what had happened spread quickly through the district.

The death of John the Baptist

1. Herod Antipas, ruler of Galilee, gave a birthday feast for his lords and captains.

2. And Salome, daughter of Herodias, his wife, danced for them. She so pleased them that Herod swore to give her anything she wished, up to half his kingdom.

3. "What shall I ask?" the girl said to her mother. Now John the Baptist had condemned Herodias for marrying her brother-in-law, and she hated him for it.

4. So she replied: "Ask for John the Baptist's head!" Because of his oath Herod could do nothing but order John's execution.

5. Salome was given the head on a dish, and took it to her mother. But Herod believed that Jesus was John come back to life.

Feeding the five thousand

1. Hearing of John's death Jesus went to a desert place, but huge crowds followed Him to be taught and healed.

2. When evening came His disciples wanted them to be sent away for food. "Feed them yourselves!" said Jesus. Andrew said: "This lad has five loaves and two fishes——

3. —but what good are they among so many?" For the crowd numbered about five thousand. "Make them sit down," said Jesus, and they did so.

4. Then Jesus took the loaves and fishes and gave thanks. He handed them to the disciples who kept breaking them and distributing them to the people. When all had eaten as much as they wanted, Jesus told the disciples to gather the fragments. Twelve baskets were filled!

Jesus walks on the sea

1. Having seen the miracle of the feeding of the five thousand with a few loaves and fishes, the people tried to take Jesus and make Him their King.

2. But He would not have it. He told His disciples to set sail for the farther shore, and Himself sent the crowds away. Then He went up into a mountain alone to pray. Meanwhile the disciples had obeyed their Master and were already some way out into the lake. But a great wind arose and they were soon in difficulties. Although they used their oars manfully, their ship was tossed about by the waves. Suddenly, in the darkness, they saw Jesus walking on the sea towards them. They were terrified, thinking Him to be a ghost. But He called to them: "Be of good cheer; do not be afraid—it is I!"

3. Peter called: "Lord, tell me to come to Thee on the water!" "Come," replied Jesus.

4. Then Peter began to walk on the water; but the rough wind made him afraid and, sinking, he cried: "Lord, save me!" Jesus took him by the hand.

5. "Why did you doubt?" He asked. And when they were in the boat the wind stopped, and the disciples worshipped Him, saying: "Truly, Thou art the Son of God!"

Jesus in Phoenicia

1. Then Jesus and His disciples left Galilee and travelled to the coasts of Tyre and Sidon in Phoenicia. Here Jesus stayed in secret, but a Syrophenician woman found the house where he was lodging.

2. And she knelt at His feet begging Him to heal her daughter who was dangerously ill. Jesus' mission was to the Jews first, so He said to her, a heathen: "Let the children first be satisfied: it is not right to take their bread and throw it to the dogs."

3. "True, Lord," she said, "but the little dogs under the table eat the children's crumbs." Jesus marveled at her witty reply and answered:

4. "You shall have your wish." And when the woman returned home she found her daughter lying on her bed but well again, as Jesus had promised.

The power that heals

1. Returning from Tyre and Sidon Jesus was met by a crowd bringing for healing a deaf and dumb man.

2. Jesus put His fingers to the man's ears, spat and touched his tongue and, looking to heaven, He sighed: "Be opened!"

3. At once the man could hear and speak plainly. Jesus ordered the people not to talk about it, but they spread the news.

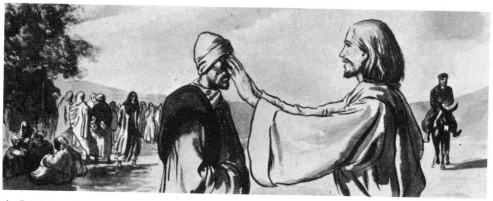

4. Later, at Bethsaida, the crowds brought Him a blind man. Jesus led the man out of the town, anointed his eyes with saliva and, having placed His hands on them, asked if he could see anything. "I see men as trees walking," he replied. Then Jesus touched him again, and he saw clearly.

Peter's confession of faith

1. Jesus now led His disciples towards Caesarea Philippi. On the way He asked: "Who do men say I am?" "One of the prophets," they said. "But who do *you* say I am?" He asked.

2. Simon Peter answered: "Thou art the Christ, the Son of the Living God." "Blessed art thou, Simon!" replied Jesus.

3. "My Father, Who is in heaven, has revealed this to you! I tell you: 'You are Peter, and on this rock I will build My Church, and the gates of hell shall not prevail against it'." And Jesus at once gave His disciples the strict warning that they should tell no one yet that He was indeed the Christ.

4. Then Jesus told them how He must journey to Jerusalem, suffer at the hands of the chief priests and scribes and be killed; but, on the third day after His death, rise again. Peter protested: "These things shall not happen to Thee, Lord."

5. But Jesus rebuked Peter with these words: "Get behind Me, Satan; for you think not of the things of God, but only of the things of man." Then He turned to them all, and said: "If any man wants to come after Me, let him take up his cross and follow Me. Whoever will lose his life for My sake, shall find it."

The Transfiguration

Six days later, Jesus led Peter, James and John up into the mountains. There He prayed; and as He did so, they saw His face become as bright as the sun and His garments shining white. Then Moses and Elijah, the two great prophets, appeared and spoke with Him. Peter cried: "Master, let us make tabernacles, one for Thee, one for Moses and one for Elijah." As he spoke, a bright cloud overshadowed them and a voice said: "This is My beloved Son; hear Him." Greatly afraid, the disciples fell on their faces, and when they looked up again Jesus was alone. As they came down the mountain-side, He commanded them not to tell anyone yet what they had seen.

"Help Thou mine unbelief"

1. When Jesus came down from the mountain, He saw His other disciples surrounded by crowds. A man ran to Him crying: "Master, have mercy on my son here for he suffers from fits of madness and Thy disciples could not cure him!" "O, faithless generation!" sighed Jesus. "How long shall I be with you?"

2. The boy fell down in a fit. The people thought he was dead, but Jesus turned to his father. "All things are possible if only you believe," He said.

3. Weeping, the man cried: "Lord, I believe—help Thou mine unbelief!" Then Jesus took the boy by the hand and he got up, sane and well.

The greatest
in God's Kingdom

1. Jesus and His disciples then made their way back to Capernaum, travelling through Galilee. While they were on their journey, the disciples began disputing among themselves as to which of them should be the greatest in the Kingdom of Heaven.

2. When they reached Capernaum, Jesus asked them: "What was it you disputed among yourselves while we were on the way here?" They would not tell Him. Then Jesus said: "If anyone wishes to be great, he must first humble himself and serve everyone." Then, gathering His disciples around Him——

3. —He took a child in His arms and said: "Whoever shall become as lowly and simple as this little child shall be the greatest in the Kingdom of Heaven. And whoever accepts and cares for such a child in My name accepts Me, too; and whoever accepts Me accepts not Me alone but Him who sent Me."

Jesus in the midst

And after He had taught them this, Jesus told the disciples that if two or three people united in prayer on earth to ask anything of their Father in heaven, He would grant it. "For," said Jesus, "where two or three are gathered together in My name, there am I in the midst of them."

The ungrateful servant

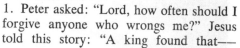

1. Peter asked: "Lord, how often should I forgive anyone who wrongs me?" Jesus told this story: "A king found that—

2. "—one of his servants was greatly in his debt, and ordered that the man and all he had should be sold for payment. The man begged for mercy.

3. "So the king, in pity, freed him and forgave the debt. Then that servant went to another, who owed him a few pounds, and demanded his money.

4. "He refused the man time to pay and sent him to prison. When the king heard of this he cried to the ungrateful servant: 'Wicked man! I forgave your debt.'

5. "Angrily he ordered the servant to be punished until payment was made. So," said Jesus, "shall God do to you if you do not also freely forgive."

73

The thunderers

1. Jesus told His disciples again that He must go to Jerusalem to die, and steadfastly set His face towards the city.

2. Among those who followed were James and John, to whom Jesus gave the nickname "the thunderbolts." This is how it happened. A certain Samaritan village would not receive Him, knowing that He would not stay with them but would go on to the Jews.

3. So the brothers cried angrily: "Lord, shall we command fire to come down from heaven to burn them up?" Jesus rebuked them with these words:

4. "The Son of Man has not come into the world to destroy men's lives, but to save them." And they went on to stay at another village.

The cost of discipleship

1. On the way to Jerusalem a certain scribe came to Jesus and said to Him: "Master, I will follow Thee wherever Thou goest." But Jesus replied: "Foxes have holes, and the birds of the air have nests—but the Son of Man has no place where He can lay His head."

2. To another disciple, who wished to stay at home until his father died, Jesus said: "Follow Me! Let the spiritually dead bury the dead." To a third, who wanted to say goodbye to his family before following Him, our Lord said: "No man who looks back once he has put his hand to the plough is fit for God's kingdom."

"The Light of the World"

1. Jesus' kinsmen urged Him to claim publicly in Jerusalem that He was the Messiah.

2. For they knew the city would be full of people celebrating the Feast of the Tabernacles, the harvest festival. Knowing they did not really believe, Jesus refused to go to the feast with them; but He later went quietly by Himself. Later, He began to teach in the Temple.

3. And everyone marvelled at His sayings. Some believed Him to be the Messiah. Then the chief priests and Pharisees sent officers to take Him.

4. But the officers would not arrest Jesus, and returned without Him, saying: "No man ever spoke like this Man." "Are you also deceived?" asked the Pharisees.

5. Jesus spoke again to the people in the Temple: "I am the Light of the World; whoever follows Me shall not walk in darkness, but shall have the light of life." Then He told them that He spoke as He had been taught by God, and that whoever kept His word——

6. —would never die. At this they grew angry, for they thought that Jesus set Himself above the prophets and Abraham. Jesus replied: "Before Abraham began to be, I AM." And they took up stones to throw at Him, but Jesus hid Himself and went out of the Temple, passing calmly through them.

A sinful woman

1. As Jesus sat teaching in the Temple, the scribes and Pharisees brought a sinful woman to Him, saying: "Moses' Law commands she should be stoned. What sayest Thou?" They said this in the hope that His reply would give them evidence to accuse Him. But Jesus stooped and wrote on the ground as though He had not heard them.

2. They questioned Him until at last He looked up: "Let him among you who is without sin cast the first stone!" And they were ashamed, and went out one by one.

3. When Jesus found the woman was alone, He asked: "Has no man condemned you?" "No man, Lord." "Neither do I condemn you: go, and sin no more," He said.

The man born blind

1. Seeing by the way a beggar blind from birth, Jesus anointed his eyes with clay made with spittle and said: "Wash in the Pool of Siloam."

2. The man obeyed and his sight was restored. When he told neighbors Jesus had cured him, they took him to the Pharisees for questioning.

3. Then when they heard him say that Jesus was a prophet, and had healed him, they brought him to his parents to ask if he were indeed born blind.

4. "Yes," they said. But they were afraid that they would be turned out of the synagogue if they agreed that Jesus was the Messiah. The Pharisees however——

5. —did thrust their son out, for he argued that only one sent from God could have opened his eyes. He found Jesus, and cried: "Lord, I believe!"

The Good Shepherd

1. Jesus, in His teaching, described Himself as the Good Shepherd and His faithful followers as a flock of sheep.

2. "When a wolf comes to attack the flock," said Jesus, "the man who does not own the sheep, but who has been hired to look after them, leaves them and runs away. He does this because, as a hireling, he does not really care for them. Then the wolf catches the sheep and scatters them.

3. "But I am the Good Shepherd, and the Good Shepherd gives up his life for the sheep. I know My sheep and My sheep know Me, even as My heavenly Father knows Me and I know My heavenly Father.

4. "I have other sheep, which are not in this fold. Them also I must bring into the fold; and they shall hear My voice. Then there shall be only one flock and only one Shepherd. No man takes My life from Me, but I lay it down Myself so that I can take it again."

The good Samaritan

1. A lawyer asked Jesus: "What shall I do to gain eternal life?" In turn Jesus asked him what the Law of Moses laid down. "Love God with all your heart, soul, strength and mind, and your neighbor as yourself," he answered.

2. "Do this and you will live," replied Jesus. "And who is my neighbor?" asked the lawyer. Then Jesus told him the story of a man, travelling from Jerusalem to Jericho, who was attacked by thieves, stripped of his clothes, wounded by them and left half dead.

3. By chance a Jewish priest came that way. When he saw the wounded man lying in the road, he passed by on the other side.

4. Soon after, a Jewish minister passed the same way. He went up and looked at the wounded man, and then he too passed by.

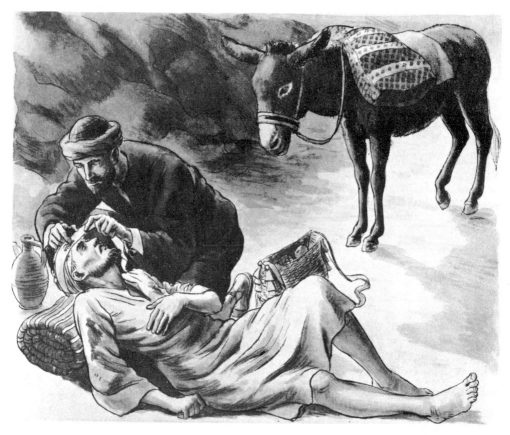

5. "But a certain Samaritan," said Jesus, knowing the Jews hated the Samaritans, "came to where he lay, and had compassion on him. He bound up his wounds, bathing them with oil and wine, set him on his own beast, brought him to an inn, and cared for him.

6. "When he left he told the landlord: 'Take care of this man, and I will pay whatever you spend on him when I return.'

7. "Which, then, was neighbor?" asked Jesus. "He who showed mercy," replied the lawyer. "Go—and do the same," Jesus said.

Martha and Mary

1. Jesus and His disciples came to Bethany, to the house of a woman named Martha, who received Him into her home. She had a sister, Mary, who sat and listened to Jesus' teaching.

2. But Martha, worried about so much work, came to Jesus, saying: "Lord, dost Thou not care that Mary has left me to serve alone? Tell her to help me." Jesus replied: "Martha, you worry about serving Me in worldly things. Mary chooses to serve Me in things of the spirit. This service shall not be taken from her."

The rich fool

1. "A man's life," said Jesus, "does not consist in the amount of his possessions." He told the story of a rich man whose land produced a greater harvest than he had room to store.

2. So he thought to himself: "I will pull down my barns and build bigger ones, and there I will store all my crops and my goods.

3. "And I will say to my soul: 'Soul, you have many goods laid up for many years; take your ease, eat, drink and be merry.'"

4. But God said to him: "You fool, this night your soul shall be demanded from you. Who, then, shall own these things which you have stored?" Then to His disciples Jesus added: "Just such a man is he who stores treasure for himself, but is not rich towards God. Therefore, I say to you: 'Do not be anxious about life'."

Worldly anxiety

"Have no undue thought," Jesus taught again, "for clothes or food. God feeds the birds, which do not sow nor reap. Are you not more precious to Him than they? Look at the wild flowers. They do not work nor spin. Yet even Solomon, in all his glory, was never dressed like one of them. Your heavenly Father knows you need food and clothes, and if you seek first God's kingdom and the right way of living, they shall be given to you."

Watching for the Master's coming

1. The disciples of Jesus are bidden to be always ready for His coming, for He comes when we least expect Him.

2. They should be like the watchful servant of a master who returns at night from a wedding; their lamps are lit, and they are at once ready to open the door, no matter how late it is, when their master knocks. Then the master shows his pleasure by making them sit together for a meal, and serves them himself.

3. Or being a disciple is like being a steward set over a household. How happy he is to be found caring for the servants when the master comes.

4. But if such a steward should get drunk in his master's absence, and ill-treat those under him, he will suffer when the master suddenly returns.

Healing on
the Sabbath

1. In a synagogue one Sabbath, Jesus called to Him a woman who for eighteen years had been bowed and crippled.

2. Laying His hand on her He said: "Woman, you are loosed from your infirmity." At once she stood upright, praising God. The ruler of the synagogue protested that people should not come for healing on the Sabbath. "But on the Sabbath you loose your ox or ass for water—ought not this woman to be loosed from her bond?" said Jesus.

"I and My Father are One"

1. During the Feast of the Dedication of the Temple in the winter, Jesus was again in Jerusalem, and He walked in Solomon's porch in the Temple. Some of the people came to Him, saying: "How long are we to be in suspense? Tell us if Thou art the Christ!"

2. Jesus said: "Why do you not believe what I tell you? The works I do in My Father's name bear witness of Me. My sheep hear My voice and they follow Me, and I give them eternal life. No man shall take them from Me. My Father gave them to Me and no one can take them from Him. I and My Father are One."

3. At once the Jews took up stones to stone Him. But He said calmly: "I have done many good works for My Father: for which of them do you stone Me?" They answered: "Not for good works, but for blasphemy, because Thou, being a man, makest Thyself God!"

4. And when they tried to take Jesus, He escaped from them and went to the place beyond Jordan where John the Baptist first baptized. There He stayed for a time. Many people followed Him there, and believed in Him, saying: "John performed no miracle, but all that he told us about this Man was true."

Lament over Jerusalem

1. When certain Pharisees warned Jesus to leave because Herod would kill Him, He answered:

2. "Go and tell that fox that I will do My work here until it is finished! A prophet must not die away from Jerusalem. O, Jerusalem, Jerusalem, that stones and kills them sent to you, how often would I have gathered your children together as a hen gathers her brood under her wings—but you would not!"

The true disciple

1. "Unless a man forsakes all," said Jesus, "he cannot be My disciple. A certain man," He went on, "prepared a feast and sent his servants to bring in the guests. But they all began to make excuses for not coming.

2. " 'I have bought some land and must go and see it,' said one.

3. " 'I have bought five yoke of oxen and am going to test them,' said another.

4. " 'I have married a wife and so cannot come,' said a third.

5. "When the man heard these excuses, he was angry. 'Go into the city streets and bring in the poor, the maimed, the lame and the blind,' he said.

6. "When there was yet room he ordered: 'Go to the highways and hedges and compel them to come. None of the invited guests shall ever taste my food!'

7. "You see," said Jesus, "being a disciple is like a man building a tower. He first counts the cost to see whether he has sufficient to finish it lest men mock him, saying: 'This man began to build but could not finish.'

8. "Or it is like being a king who is about to go to war. First he considers whether his forces can defeat the enemy.

9. "Or else, while the army of the enemy king is still far off, he decides to send ambassadors to sue for peace.

10. "To be My disciple," Jesus added, "a man must give up everything he has, even those he loves the best—his wife, his children, and all his family. He must even be prepared to give up life itself; for anyone who does not carry his cross and follow Me is not worthy to be My disciple."

The lost sheep

1. Jesus taught the Pharisees that a sinner who repents gives more joy in heaven than all those good people who think they have no need to repent. "If a shepherd loses one sheep from his flock," He said——

2. "—he immediately leaves all his other sheep and goes out to look for the lost one. And when he has found it, he lays it on his shoulder.

3. "Then, when he comes home, he calls his friends and neighbors together, saying: 'Rejoice with me, for I have found my lost sheep.'"

The lost coin

1. To illustrate the same point in His teaching, Jesus spoke again by parable: "What woman is there," He said, "having ten pieces of silver who, if she loses one, does not light a candle and sweep the house, seeking diligently until she finds it?

2. "And when she has found it, she calls her friends and her neighbors together saying: 'Rejoice with me, for I have found the piece of silver which I had lost!' There is joy like that among the angels of God," said Jesus, turning to the Pharisees who were listening, "over one sinner who repents!"

The lost son

1. Another story Jesus told was that of a man who had two sons, the younger of whom asked him for that part of the inheritance due to him. So the father divided his possessions.

2. Not many days later the younger son went to a far country, and there wasted his wealth in riotous living.

3. Later there was a famine in that land, and he began to want. So he went to seek work. A man sent him to the fields——

4. —to look after pigs. No one gave him food, and he was so hungry he could have eaten the husks on which the pigs fed. One day he saïd to himself: "My father's servants always have enough to eat. I will go to my father and say: 'Father, I have sinned and am not worthy to be called your son. Make me a servant.'"

5. So he went back home; but while he was still a long way off his father saw him and ran and kissed him. Then the son said: "Father, I have sinned——"

6. But his father called: "Bring shoes and the best robe! And kill the fatted calf; for this my son was lost and is found!"

7. When the elder son returned from the fields, he heard music and merry-making and asked what it meant. They told him.

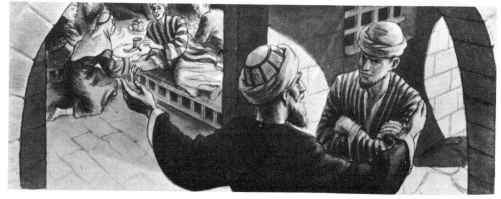

8. And he was angry and would not go in. His father came and begged him, but he exclaimed: "I have worked many years, but have never been given so much as a kid to entertain my friends!" His father replied: "Son, all I have is yours; and we ought to be glad today for your lost brother is found."

Rich man, beggar man

1. When the Pharisees mocked Jesus He told this story. "There was a rich man who wore purple and fine linen and feasted every day. At his gate lay Lazarus, a poor beggar, starving and covered with sores, who hoped to feed on crumbs that fell from the rich man's table. Both men died. Lazarus was received by Abraham into the realm of blessed life, but the rich man was judged unfit to enter there.

2. "In torment he looked up and saw Lazarus with Abraham, to whom he cried: 'Send Lazarus to comfort me!' 'Son,' said Abraham, 'there is a great gulf fixed between us which none can cross.' 'Then send him to my brothers. If one came from the dead they would repent,' he pleaded. Abraham answered: 'If they ignore Moses and the prophets they will not be persuaded—though one rise from the dead!'"

The raising of Lazarus

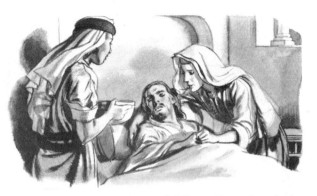

1. In Bethany lived another Lazarus, brother of Martha and Mary. Jesus loved the family; and when Lazarus was ill his sisters sent word to Jesus.

2. But Jesus stayed where He was for two days. Then He said to His disciples: "Lazarus sleeps; but I go to wake him out of the sleep of death.

3. "Let us go into Judea again." Thomas, remembering that the Jews had tried to stone Jesus there, said: "Let us also go, that we may die with Him."

4. As Jesus came towards Bethany, Martha met Him, saying: "Lord, our brother would not have died if Thou hadst been here." "Your brother shall rise again," Jesus answered. "I know he shall rise again on the last day," she replied. Then Jesus said: "I am the Resurrection and the Life. He who believes in Me shall never die."

5. When they came to the grave, surrounded by the mourners, Jesus wept.

6. Then Jesus told them to take away the stone, and looking up to heaven, He prayed.

7. After this, He called out in a loud voice: "Lazarus, come forth!" And Lazarus stumbled out, bound as he was with the grave clothes. "Loose him," said Jesus. Then many of the Jews who were there, and had seen the miracle, believed that Jesus was the Messiah, whom God should send into the world.

8. But others went to the Pharisees to tell them what Jesus had done, and the Pharisees and chief priests held a council. "If we leave this man alone," they said, "the people will believe Him and the Romans destroy us." But Caiaphas said: "It is better for us rather that this one man should die than that the whole nation should perish."

The ten lepers

1. Passing through Samaria on the way to Jerusalem, Jesus was outside a village one day when ten lepers called to Him.

2. They stood some distance away, crying: "Master, have mercy on us!" Jesus said to them: "Go and show yourselves to the priests" (for only the priests could certify them healed). And as they went on their way, they discovered that they were clean again.

3. One of them, when he found he was healed, turned back and fell at Jesus' feet, giving Him thanks. "Were there not ten cleansed?" observed Jesus. "Yet only one returns to give glory to God, and he is a Samaritan." Then to the man: "Go your way; your faith has made you whole."

The proud and the humble

1. To people who were too confident in their own goodness and despised others, Jesus said: "Two men went up into the Temple to pray. One was a Pharisee and the other a tax-gatherer. The Pharisee prayed like this: 'God, I thank Thee that I am not as other men are!

2. "'I thank Thee I am not as this tax-gatherer; I live according to the Law.' But the tax-gatherer, with downcast eyes, beat his breast and said:

3. "'God be merciful to me, a sinner!' I tell you," Jesus commented, "that he, rather than the other, went home cleansed of his sin. The humble shall be exalted."

The rich young ruler

1. As Jesus went on His way a rich young ruler came running and kneeled before Him, saying: "Good Master, what should I do to inherit eternal life?"

2. Jesus replied: "Why do you call Me good? Only God is good." Then he said: "You must keep the commandments."

3. The young ruler protested: "I have kept them all, ever since I was a child. What else should I do?"

4. Jesus, looking at him, loved him, and said: "There is one more thing—sell all you have and give to the poor. Then take up your cross and follow Me."

5. But when the young man heard this, he went away in sorrow, for he had great possessions. "How hard it is for a rich man to enter God's Kingdom!" said Jesus.

Jesus and the children

When little children were brought to Jesus, so that He might lay His hands on them and bless them, His disciples tried to turn them away. But Jesus said: "Do not forbid the little children to come to Me, for the Kingdom of God is made up of those who are like children. If you cannot accept the Kingdom with the heart of a child, you will never find your way into it." Then He took the children in His arms and blessed them.

The laborers in the vineyard

1. "There was a man," said Jesus, "who one day hired laborers for his vineyard.

2. "When they had agreed on wages, they began to work. Later in the morning the man hired more laborers. 'Whatever is the right wage, I will pay,' he said.

3. "He did the same at noon and at three in the afternoon. At five o'clock, finding men still idle in the market-place, he sent them to work with the same words.

4. "But those hired first complained when all received the same pay, for they thought it unfair that those who had worked one hour only should get as much as they. 'But,' said the vineyard owner, 'we agreed on the wages. I will give to the last as I have given to you!' So," said Jesus, "in God's Kingdom first and last shall be alike rewarded."

How to be great

1. As they neared Jericho on their way to Jerusalem, Jesus again told the twelve of His coming betrayal, death and resurrection. But they did not understand.

2. The mother of James and John knelt before Jesus, asking that they might have the chief thrones in His Kingdom. Jesus said to the brothers:

3. "You do not know what you ask. Are you prepared to suffer as I shall suffer?" They answered: "We are prepared." Then Jesus said:

4. "You shall indeed suffer, but thrones are not Mine to give." The other ten were indignant about James and John, but Jesus said to them: "Let him among you who wants to be the greatest, be the servant of all, for even the Son of Man has not come to be served but to serve, and to give His life as a ransom for many."

The story of Zaccheus

1. In Jericho the chief tax-gatherer was the wealthy Zaccheus. When Jesus entered the town, Zaccheus tried to see Him; but he was too short to see over the heads of the crowd.

2. So he ran and climbed a sycamore tree along the road. As Jesus came by, he looked up and said: "Zaccheus, come down!"

3. "Today I want to stay at your house," Jesus added. Zaccheus hurried down from the tree and welcomed Him joyfully.

4. Zaccheus was so moved by Jesus' visit that he promised to give half his goods to the poor, and to repay four times over the money he had wrongly taken. Jesus turned to the people, saying: "Today salvation has come to this house. The Son of Man comes to seek and save that which is lost."

The parable of the talents

1. It is important to make good use of God's gifts. "The Kingdom of Heaven," said Jesus, "is like a man who, before going to a distant country, distributed his money, giving one servant five talents, and another two, and a third one.

2. "The first two traded, until the first had received five other talents, and the second two more. Not so the man with one talent.

3. "He went and dug a hole and hid the talent in it. When the master returned he asked for an account of the money.

4. "To the first two he said: 'Well done, good and faithful servants; because you have been loyal in few things you shall be rulers over many.'

5. "But because the third had made no use of his talent, the master cried: 'Wicked and lazy servant!' Then: 'Throw this unprofitable servant out!'"

Supper at Bethany

1. On Friday, six days before the Passover, Jesus came to Bethany, to the house of Lazarus, whom He had raised from the dead.

2. Lazarus and his sisters prepared a supper for Jesus. Lazarus sat with Him at the table and Martha served. Mary brought in to Him some costly ointment, whose perfume filled the whole house, anointed Jesus' feet and wiped them with her hair. When Judas Iscariot, one of those who sat at supper, saw this, he protested.

3. "If this ointment had been sold, it would have brought in a large sum of money to give to the poor!" he said indignantly.

4. But Jesus replied: "Let her alone. You will always have the poor among you, but not me." The Sabbath (Saturday) He spent quietly at Bethany.

Palm Sunday

1. On the first day of the next week—our Sunday—Jesus went to Jerusalem. From the Mount of Olives He saw the city and wept over it. Then He said to two disciples: "Go into that village, and you will find a young colt tied. Bring it to Me."

4. Then was fulfilled the prophecy of Christ's entry into Jerusalem. The crowds of pilgrims for the Passover waved palm branches and shouted: "Hosanna to the Son of David! Blessed is He that comes in the name of the Lord!" The children were there, too, crying: "Hosanna in the highest!"

112

2. They found the colt and, when challenged, answered as He had told them: "The Lord has need of him."

3. It was like a password. On returning to Jesus, they laid their cloaks on the colt, and set Jesus upon it.

5. When the Temple priests protested, Jesus quoted from the Scriptures: "Out of the mouths of babes and sucklings Thou hast perfected praise."

Cleansing the Temple

1. While He was in Jerusalem, Jesus went to the Temple. The Jews, by law, were allowed to sell animals to the worshippers for their sacrifices; but Jesus found the court of the sacred Temple turned into a noisy market, and the people cheated in the exchange of money.

2. The Temple was full of cattle and sheep, and men were buying and selling and changing coins. When Jesus saw the turmoil, He made a whip of small cords, and drove them all out, scattered the changers' money, and overthrew their tables. To those who sold doves, He said: "Take them away!

3. "Do not make My Father's house a market-place!" When the Jews demanded a sign of His authority, He replied:

4. "Destroy this Temple, and in three days I will raise it up." In saying this, Jesus spoke of His death and resurrection.

"By what authority?"

1. As Jesus taught in the Temple next morning, the elders again asked: "By what authority do you do these things?" "By what authority did John baptize?" He asked them. Now they could not agree that it was God's, since they did not believe in John.

2. Nor dared they say it was man's, since the people held John to be a prophet. "We cannot tell," they said. "Neither do I tell you My authority," said Jesus.

3. He told them of a man who ordered his two sons to work in his vineyard. The first refused, but later repented, and went. The second said he would, but did not.

4. "Which of the two, therefore," Jesus asked, "did what the father wished?" The elders had to answer: "The first." "Just so," said Jesus, "tax-gatherers and sinful women go into the Kingdom of God before you; for they do afterwards repent, and believe."

The royal wedding feast

1. "The Kingdom of Heaven," said Jesus, again, "is like the marriage festival which a king arranged for his son. When all was ready he sent servants to tell the guests to come to the wedding.

2. "They would not, so the king sent again. But they rejected his invitation——

3. "—and made light of it, one going to his farm and another to his merchandise.

4. "Others would not let the servants go but beat them and killed them.

5. "When the king heard what had happened, he was so angry that he sent out his armies against the murderers, destroyed them and burned their city. Then he said to his servants: 'The wedding feast is now ready but the guests were unfit to be invited.

6. " 'Go out into the streets and gather together all those you can find and invite them to the marriage.' So the servants obeyed him and brought in to the feast as wedding guests both good and bad alike."

The wicked tenants

1. Jesus told another parable of a man who planted and hedged a vineyard, put in a winepress and let it to tenants.

2. When the grapes were ripe, he sent servants to collect some of the fruit as rent. But the tenants beat or stoned them. Some of them were even killed.

3. Then the man sent his son, saying: "Surely they will respect my son." But the tenants slew the son also, saying: "Let us kill him and seize his inheritance."

4. Then Jesus said: "What will the owner of the vineyard do when he comes?" "Destroy them, and let the vineyard to others," they replied. "That is why I warn you that the Kingdom of God will be taken from you and given to those who will produce the fruits," said Jesus, meaning that it would be taken from the Jews and given to others.

Tribute to Caesar

1. The Pharisees and the Herodians, the religious and political parties among the Jews, were determined to trap Jesus so that they could put Him to death. So they sent spies, saying: "Master, we know Thou truthfully teachest the way of God, without fearing any man; tell us, is it right to pay taxes to Caesar of Rome, or not?" Jesus saw their craftiness.

2. If He said "Yes," the Pharisees would denounce Him to the people; if He said "No," the Herodians would denounce Him to the Romans. "You hypocrites!" He replied. "Give me a coin! Now, whose is this head and inscription?" "Caesar's," they replied. "Give then to Caesar the things that are Caesar's—and to God the things that are God's!"

"The greatest commandment"

1. Then one of the Pharisees, a scribe learned in the sacred Law, asked Jesus this question: "Master, which is the greatest commandment in the Law?"

2. Jesus answered: " 'The Lord Our God is one Lord, and thou shalt love the Lord with all thy heart, with all thy soul, with all thy mind and with all thy strength.'

3. "This is the first and greatest commandment. The second is like it: 'Thou shalt love thy neighbor as thyself.' There is no commandment greater than these."

4. "Indeed, Master, Thou hast spoken the truth," replied the scribe, "for these are worth more than all the burnt offerings and sacrifices." Jesus, seeing he answered wisely, added: "You are not far from the Kingdom of God."

The widow's mite

1. As Jesus sat near the Temple treasure-chest, He warned His disciples against the scribes. "They love to parade in long robes, and to receive respectful greetings in public," He said. "They seek the best places in the synagogues and at feasts; but they rob poor widows and their prayer is a mockery." As He spoke a poor widow came by.

2. She threw into the chest two mites (which make a farthing). "You see," said Jesus, "that poor widow gave more to the treasury than all the others; for they threw in some of their abundance, but she, though in need herself, gave all that she had."

"I will draw all men unto Me"

1. Certain Greeks, who were worshipping at the Passover Feast, asked to see Jesus. When Philip and Andrew asked Him, He answered: "The hour has come——

2. "—for the Son of Man to be glorified. Unless a grain of wheat falls into the ground and dies, it remains alone; if it dies, it produces many others.

3. "Father, glorify Thy name!" Then a voice came from heaven: "I have and I will." Some of the people said it thundered; others, that an angel spoke to Him.

4. Jesus went on: "Now shall the Prince of this world be cast out! And I, if I be lifted up from the earth, will draw all men unto Me!" He knew how He would die.

Destruction
of the Temple

1. As they left the Temple, one of the disciples praised the magnificent building.

2. Jesus cried: "The days will come when not one stone shall be left standing on the other!" That night, on the Mount of Olives, Peter, James, Andrew and John asked Him privately: "When shall this happen? And how shall we know of Thy coming?" Then Jesus warned them.

3. There would be wars and rumors of wars; nation would rise against nation, kingdom against kingdom. These things must come; but they were not the end.

4. For there would be famines, pestilences and earthquakes, great distress in the land, wretchedness for all the people. But these were only the beginning of sorrows.

5. "Take heed that you are not deceived for many false prophets shall come in My name, and shall be believed.

6. "But he who endures to the end shall be saved; and this same gospel shall be preached in all countries.

7. "But look after yourselves," Jesus went on, "for you will often be betrayed. Then they will persecute you, bringing you before kings and rulers, beating you in the synagogues, casting you into prison, and even condemning you to death; you will be hated for My sake. But I will give you words to answer them."

8. Terrible destruction would come, and the heathen would desecrate Jerusalem, as the prophets foretold. When armies surrounded the city, the people of Judea should flee to the mountains. Those days would be the days of vengeance.

124

The wise and foolish maidens

1. One must always be ready for the Kingdom of Heaven. "Ten bridesmaids went out at night to meet the bridegroom," said Jesus. "And as they waited they fell asleep.

2. "Five were wise, and carried spare oil for their lamps; but five were foolish, and did not. When they were called, the lamps of the foolish were out.

3. "They asked the wise for oil, but were told: 'We have not brought enough. Go quickly and buy some!' Then those who were ready went to the marriage.

4. "And the door was shut. When the foolish came back, they cried: 'Lord, Lord, open the door and let us in!'

5. "But the bridegroom replied: 'I do not know you!' So keep watch, for you never know when the Son of Man is coming!'

125

The Last

1. "For when the Son of Man shall come in His glory, and all the holy angels with Him, then shall He sit upon His glorious throne, and before Him shall be gathered

2. "Then will the King say to them on His right hand: 'Come, you whom my Father has blessed! Inherit the kingdom prepared for you from the foundation of the world. For I was hungry, and you gave Me food; thirsty, and you gave Me drink; a stranger, and you took Me in. I was naked, and you clothed Me; sick, and you visited Me; in prison, and you came to Me.' Then shall the righteous say: 'Lord, when?' And the King shall answer: 'Inasmuch as you have done it unto one of the least of these My brothers, you have done it unto Me!'

Judgment

all nations. He shall separate them one from another as a shepherd divides the sheep from the goats, the sheep on His right hand, but the goats on His left hand.

3. "To those on the left He will say: 'Depart from Me, you who are accursed, to the everlasting fire prepared for the devil and his angels. I was hungry, and you gave Me no food; thirsty, and you gave Me no drink; a stranger, and you did not take Me in; I was naked, and you did not clothe Me; sick, and in prison, and you did not visit Me.' Then shall they also answer: 'Lord, when did we see Thee hungry or thirsty, a stranger, or naked, or sick, or in prison?' And he will reply: 'Inasmuch as you did it not to one of the least of these you did it not unto Me.' "

Judas sells his soul

1. Then Jesus said to His apostles: "In two days' time it is the Feast of the Passover. The Son of Man is going to be betrayed to be crucified."

2. Now the chief priests, scribes and elders of the people held a meeting at the palace of Caiaphas, the high-priest. They consulted together as to how they might take Jesus quietly, and kill Him. It must not be done on the Feast Day in case there should be an uproar among the people.

3. But Judas Iscariot, one of the Twelve, went to them, and said: "What will you give me if I hand Jesus over to you?"

4. They bargained with him for thirty pieces of silver. And from that time Judas looked for the chance to betray Jesus.

The Last Supper

1. On Thursday, the day before the Passover, Jesus sent Peter and John into the city, saying: "Meet a man carrying a pitcher of water. Follow him to his house and say, 'The Master asks: Where is the guest-chamber where I shall eat the Passover with My disciples?'

2. "He will show you a large upper room. There make ready for us." The disciples went and did as He had said; and in the evening Jesus sat at supper with them.

3. But the disciples had again been quarrelling as to who was the greatest among them, and should therefore sit nearest to Him. Jesus rose from the table.

4. He poured water into a basin, and began to wash the disciples' feet. Peter protested: "Lord, dost Thou wash my feet?" "If I do not wash you, you have nothing in common with Me," Jesus replied. "Lord, not my feet only, then, but my hands and my head!"

"Is it I?"

1. After Jesus had sat down again, He said: "Do you realize what I have done? You call Me Master and Lord—and I have washed your feet! In this I have given you an example that you should do as I have done to you. The servant is not greater than his Lord."

2. Peter, unable to bear the suspense, signalled to John, the disciple whom Jesus loved: "Ask Him who it is." John leaned his head back.

3. He whispered: "Lord, who is it?" "One to whom I give the sop," answered Jesus. Then He gave them each in turn a piece of bread dipped in the dish of herbs.

130

There was silence for a moment. The disciples began to feel very ashamed. Then He spoke words which cut to their hearts: "One of you will betray Me!" They looked at one another, wondering of whom He spoke, and each of them said to himself: "Is it I? Is it I?"

4. Still none of them knew; but John afterwards remembered that He gave first to Judas Iscariot. "What you are going to do, do quickly," Jesus said to Judas.

5. They thought Jesus was telling Judas, who looked after their money, to go and buy the food they needed. Judas went out immediately; and it was night.

The Lord's Supper

1. And as they were eating, Jesus took the bread and the wine, and He gave thanks and blessed them.

2. He broke the bread in pieces, and gave it to the disciples. "Take this and eat," He said. "This is My body, which is broken for you; do this in remembrance of Me."

3. And He took the cup and gave it to them, saying: "Drink, all of you. This cup is the new covenant in My blood, which is shed for many for the remission of sins.

4. "Drink in remembrance of Me; for I shall not drink with you again until I do so in My Father's Kingdom. You have stood loyally by Me in My trials. Now I assign you power to rule, just as My Father has given Me. You may eat and drink at My table in My Kingdom." And when they had sung a psalm, they went out to the Mount of Olives.

Peter's confidence

1. As they went their way, Jesus said to the disciples: "In a little while I must leave you. So now I give you a new commandment—that you love one another as I have loved you.

2. "By this shall all men know you are My disciples. Let not your heart be troubled; you believe in God, believe also in Me. I go to prepare a place for you; but if I go, I will come again and receive you unto Myself, that where I am, there you may be also. You know where I am going, and you know the way." Peter said:

3. "Lord, where goest Thou? I am ready to go with Thee to prison or death." Jesus replied: "I go where you cannot follow Me now; but you shall do so later.

4. "And I tell you that this night, before the cock crows, you will deny Me three times!" "Lord, even if I should die, I will not deny Thee!" cried Peter.

133

5. Then Thomas, too, said to Jesus: "Lord, we do not know where Thou goest: how can we know the way?"

6. Jesus said to him: "I am the Way, the Truth and the Life; no one comes to the Father but by Me."

7. Philip spoke: "Lord, show us the Father." "Have I been so long with you, and yet you have not known Me, Philip? He who has seen Me, has seen the Father."

8. Jesus went on: "I am the Vine, you are the branches. My Father is the vine-grower, and He takes away every branch in Me that is unfruitful. Every fruitful branch——

9. "—He prunes, to bring forth more fruit. Abide in Me, and I will abide in you. Greater love has no man than this: that a man lay down his life for his friends. Now, let him who has purse or wallet take it, and him who has no sword, sell his cloak and buy one." "Lord," they said eagerly, "here are two swords!" "Enough, enough!" He answered.

134

Gethsemane

1. Crossing the brook Kidron, they climbed up the Mount of Olives to a garden called Gethsemane. Inside the gate Jesus left most of His disciples, saying: "Sit here, while I go over there to pray."

2. Then, with only Peter, James and John, Jesus went on deeper into the darkness of the garden and, as He did so, began to be full of terror and perplexity. He turned to the three, saying: "My heart is full of deathly sorrow. Stay here and watch with Me." Then He went on about a stone's throw, and fell on the ground and prayed:

3. "O, My Father, if it be possible, let this cup pass from Me; nevertheless, not what I will, but what Thou wilt, be done." And an angel appeared and strengthened Him.

4. Being in an agony, Jesus prayed even more intensely, and His sweat was like great drops of blood falling down to the ground. Then He arose from prayer.

5. He found the three disciples asleep. Jesus said to Peter as he awoke: "Were you not strong enough to watch with Me one hour?" Then, to them all: "Be on your guard so that you do not fall into temptation; your spirit indeed is willing, but your flesh is weak."

6. A second and yet a third time He prayed: "O, My Father, if this cup may not pass away from Me unless I drink it, Thy will be done." Again the heavy-eyed disciples were asleep. Jesus woke them. "Rise up!" He said. "The hour has come. Look, he who betrays Me is coming!" As He spoke, the Temple officers, led by Judas Iscariot, came towards them.

136

7. Now Judas had agreed on a signal with the officers that the Man whom he kissed was to be arrested. He kissed Jesus.

8. As he did so, he said: "Master, Master!" Jesus said to Judas: "Do you betray the Son of Man with a kiss?"

9. As the Temple guard seized Jesus, Peter drew his sword, struck at the high-priest's servant, Malchus, and cut off his right ear. Jesus commanded Peter:

10. "Put up your sword! My Father could send Me twelve legions of angels, but how then should the Scriptures be fulfilled that this must be?" And He healed Malchus' ear.

11. Jesus turned to the chief-priests and the Temple officers: "Do you come out armed with clubs and swords to take Me as though I were a thief? I taught daily in the Temple, but you never attempted to arrest Me there! But this is your hour of triumph, and the writings of the prophets must be fulfilled." Then all the disciples forsook Him and fled.

The trial of Jesus

1. The soldiers bound Jesus, and brought Him to Annas, father-in-law of Caiaphas, the high-priest. Annas asked Him what He taught. "I spoke openly in the Temple, where the Jews worship continually," Jesus said.

2. "Why do you ask Me?" Jesus went on. "Ask them who heard Me; they know what I said." As He spoke, one of the officers standing by Him struck Him.

3. "Is that the way to answer the high-priest?" he cried. Jesus said to him: "If I lied, you can denounce Me; but if I spoke the truth, why do you strike Me?"

4. Annas sent Jesus to Caiaphas. Peter followed, and so did John, who, as he was known to the high-priest, went into the palace. He spoke to the girl at the door——

5. —and brought Peter in from outside. The girl looked at Peter. "Surely you, also, are one of this Man's disciples?" she said. "Woman, I am not!" Peter answered her.

6. Caiaphas and the Sanhedrin now began to seek evidence on some charge against Jesus by which they could condemn Him to death according to their law; but even their false witnesses could not agree.

7. Caiaphas at last asked Jesus if He had anything to say, but He did not speak. "*Art* Thou the Christ, the Son of God?" he asked. "I am," Jesus answered.

8. "And you shall see the Son of Man sitting on the right hand of power, coming in clouds of heaven." At this the high-priest rent his clothes, crying:

9. "Do we need any other witnesses? You have heard this blasphemy from His own mouth!" They all agreed: "He is guilty, and the penalty is—death!"

10. Now Peter was still outside with the servants and soldiers round the fire. A maid came in and, when she saw him, said to the others: "This is one of them!"

11. "I am not," Peter said. Then one of the men challenged him. "You're a Galilean—your accent betrays you!" Another interjected: "Did I not see you with Him in the garden?" Peter swore: "Man, I don't know what you're talking about!"

12. Meanwhile, they had led Jesus away to await the dawn, when a full meeting of the Court could be held to confirm the sentence of death. The servants mocked Him and, having blindfolded Him, they struck Him, saying: "Prophesy, Christ! Who hit Thee?"

13. The cock crew. It was dawn on Friday (our Good Friday). As they dragged Jesus through the hall, He turned and looked at Peter, who recalled His words: "Before the cock crows, you will deny Me three times!"

14. Peter ran out and wept bitterly. The Jews hurried their prisoner off to the Roman governor's palace.

The end of Judas

1. When Judas saw that Jesus had been condemned, he was in despair about what he had done.

2. He brought back to the chief-priests and elders the thirty pieces of silver he had received for betraying Jesus, and said:

3. "I have sinned! I have betrayed innocent blood!" "What is that to us?" they replied. "That is your responsibility."

4. Judas thereupon threw the silver on the Temple floor, and rushed out and hanged himself. The chief-priests would not keep the money for the Temple treasury.

5. "It is not lawful: it is the price of blood," they said. So they bought the potter's field, outside the city, to bury strangers in. It became known as "the field of blood."

141

Sentence of death

1. Pilate, the Roman governor, came out when the Jews brought Jesus to the palace court-yard. "Of what do you accuse this Man?" he asked them. "He has stirred up the people from Galilee to Jerusalem, setting Himself up as Christ, a King!"

2. Now Herod Antipas was in Jerusalem, so Pilate sent Jesus to the King. Herod had long wanted to see Him, and hoped He would do some miracle.

3. But as Jesus said and did nothing, Herod sent Him back to Pilate, who summoned Jesus to the judgment hall and asked Him: "Art Thou the King of the Jews?"

142

4. "I am a King," Jesus said. "But My kingdom is not of this world. I have come to show men the Kingdom of Truth."

5. "What is Truth?" Pilate said, half-scornfully. Jesus still would not answer the chief-priests' accusations.

6. Then Pilate's wife sent a message: "Have nothing to do with that innocent Man: I suffered much in a dream about Him."

7. So Pilate went out to the crowd. "I find no fault in Him at all," he declared. "But you have a custom that I release to you a prisoner at the Passover. Shall I release the 'King of the Jews'?" The priests urged on the people and they shouted: "Not this Man, but Barabbas!" Now Barabbas was a revolutionary, who had also committed a murder.

143

8. Pilate decided that Jesus should be whipped and then released. When the soldiers had scourged Him, they made Him a crown of thorns, put a reed in His right hand, and gave Him a purple robe. Then they mockingly bowed to Him, saying: "Hail, King of the Jews!"

9. Jesus was brought out still wearing the crown and the purple robe. "Behold the Man!" said Pilate. The chief-priests, the officers and the people with them cried out: "Crucify Him! Crucify Him!" "Take Him yourselves and crucify Him. I find no fault in Him at all."

10. Then the Jews said to Pilate: "We have a law, by which He ought to die, because He made Himself out to be the Son of God." When He heard this, Pilate was afraid.

11. Again he examined Jesus. "Where dost Thou come from? Thou knowest I have power to crucify Thee?" Jesus said: "Your power can come only from above."

12. Once more Pilate tried to secure Jesus' release, but Caiaphas and his followers said to him: "If you let this Man go, you will be involved in treason against Caesar. Whoever makes himself out to be a king, sets himself against the Emperor."

13. At nine o'clock in the morning Pilate brought Jesus out for the last time to the people. "Here is your 'King'!" he said. "Away with Him! Crucify Him!" they cried out. "Shall I crucify your King?" Pilate asked them. "*We* have no King but Caesar!" said Caiaphas.

14. Pilate saw that he could do nothing and that a riot was developing; so he washed his hands before the crowd, saying: "I am innocent of the blood of this good Man.

15. "This is your business!" They answered: "His blood be on us, and on our children!" Then the soldiers took Jesus, and led Him away to crucify Him.

145

The Crucifixion

1. Jesus, bearing His cross, went forth towards Calvary, the place of execution, called, in Aramaic, Golgotha.

2. But soon the soldiers had to lay hold of a man who was coming in from the country, and put the cross on him. He was Simon, from Cyrene, in North Africa.

3. A large company of weeping women followed Jesus. He turned to them: "Do not weep for Me: rather weep for yourselves and for your children."

4. Then, indicating the Roman soldiers, He went on: "If they do these things while the tree of our national life is still green what will they do when it is dead and dry?" At last they came to Calvary. There they offered Him drugged wine, but He would not take it.

5. Then they nailed Him to His cross and set it up with a thief on either side of Him. Jesus kept saying: "Father, forgive them! They know not what they do!" And over His head they nailed a board saying what had been His crime—"Jesus of Nazareth, King of the Jews."

6. When the chief-priests saw it, they sent to the governor, saying: "Do not write, 'The King of the Jews'!

7. "Write rather, 'He *said* I am King of the Jews'." "What I have written, I have written," returned Pilate curtly.

8. The soldiers, when they had each taken one of His garments—head-dress, cloak, girdle and sandals—diced for His tunic, which had been woven without seam.

9. The people and the rulers mocked at Him: "If Thou be the Son of God, then come down from the cross!" and "He saved others—Himself He cannot save!"

10. One of the thieves cursed Jesus: "Save Thyself and us!" The other rebuked him: "We are rightly suffering the penalty for our crimes: but this Man has done nothing wrong." Then, to Jesus: "Lord, when Thou comest in Thy kingdom, remember me." "Truly," said Jesus, "you shall be with Me in Paradise this very day."

11. Then He looked down where Mary, His mother, leaning on the arm of John, stood with others. "Woman," Jesus said to His mother, "behold your son!" And to John: "Behold your mother!" Then John took her away to his own home.

12. Suddenly darkness came over the land, and from the darkness came the sound of Jesus' cry: "My God, My God, why hast Thou forsaken Me?"

13. "He calls for Elijah!" said some of the watchers. Then Jesus cried: "I thirst!" One of the soldiers held a sponge, soaked in some of their own wine, to His lips.

14. After three hours of darkness, Jesus cried in triumph: "It is finished! Father, into Thy hands I commend My Spirit!" and gave up His life.

15. When the centurion, who was standing near Him, saw Jesus cry out like that and then die, he said: "Truly, this man was the Son of God!"

The Resurrection

1. Joseph of Arimathea, a wealthy member of the Sanhedrin, yet a good man who loved Jesus, begged Pilate to let him have His body. Pilate agreed as soon as he had confirmed that Jesus was really dead. The thieves had had their legs broken to ensure death——

2. —but Jesus had had His side pierced by a soldier's spear. Joseph, with Nicodemus, took down the body of Jesus from the cross, wrapped Him in fine linen, and laid Him in his own tomb, hewn from rock, in a nearby garden. Mary Magdalene, Salome, the mother of James and John, and Mary, the mother of James the Less and Joses, watched them.

3. Joseph and Nicodemus rolled a great stone against the entrance to the tomb; then they all went away. The next day was the Jewish Sabbath.

4. But the Jews remembered that Jesus had said: "After three days I shall rise again." So they sealed the tomb, and set a guard over it.

150

5. At dawn on the first day of the week—our Sunday—the women came with spices to embalm Jesus' body. "Who will roll the stone away from the sepulchre for us?" they said as they went. But the stone had already been rolled aside, and the tomb was—empty!

6. Mary Magdalene ran off to tell the apostles, but the other women went into the sepulchre. The body of Jesus had gone, but sitting there was a young man in shining white, who said: "Why do you seek for the living among the dead? Jesus has risen as He said. Go, tell His disciples: 'He is risen from the dead!' He is going before you into Galilee."

7. In fear and joy the women ran off with their glad news. Meanwhile, Mary had told Peter and John: "They have taken away the Lord out of the sepulchre, and we do not know where they have laid Him." The two ran to the tomb and went into the sepulchre where they saw the linen clothes lying.

8. They went away, wondering; but Mary stayed outside, weeping. Someone was by her. He asked her quietly: "Woman, why do you weep? Whom do you seek?"

9. She, thinking it was the gardener, said through her tears: "Sir, if you have carried Him off from here, tell me where you have laid Him, and *I* will take Him away."

10. Jesus said softly: "Mary." "My Master!" she cried. "Do not cling to Me," said Jesus, "for I have not yet ascended to My Father. But go to My brothers——

11. "—and tell them: 'I ascend to My Father and your Father'." Jesus also spoke to the other women going on their way. But the disciples could not believe them.

The soldiers bribed

1. Afterwards it became known what had happened at the guarded tomb during the night.

2. The earth had quaked, and an angel, whose face dazzled like lightning, and whose robe glistened like snow, had rolled the stone away from the entrance and sat on it.

3. The terrified soldiers shook with fear at the sight and fainted, lying as though they were dead. When they recovered, they ran to the city to tell Caiaphas.

4. Caiaphas called some of the Sanhedrin together, and they decided to bribe the soldiers to give a false explanation: "Say: 'His disciples came by night and stole the body while we slept.' And if this comes to the governor's ears, we will persuade him, and see that you are safe." The guards obeyed; and their account became the usual explanation among the Jews.

The Emmaus road

1. Later in the afternoon of the same day, two disciples walking home to Emmaus (a village about eight miles from Jerusalem) were overtaken by Jesus, though they did not know who it was. He asked them: "What makes you so sad?"

2. One of them, Cleophas, answered: "Are you a stranger in Jerusalem that you have not heard that Jesus of Nazareth, Whom we expected to redeem Israel——

3. "—has been crucified? His body has gone from the tomb; and some of our women-folk say that angels have said He is alive." Then Jesus quoted the Scriptures.

4. He showed how it was written that the Messiah had to suffer before He entered into glory. When they came to Emmaus, the disciples persuaded Him to stay with them.

5. As He sat at supper there, He took the bread and blessed it, and broke it and gave it to them. Then they saw and knew Who it really was; but He vanished from sight.

154

"He is risen indeed"

1. "Did not our hearts glow within us while He was talking with us!" they said to one another: and at once hurried back to Jerusalem to tell the apostles and other disciples their news. They were saying: "The Lord has risen indeed, and has appeared to Peter!"

2. Then the two told how Jesus had joined them on the road, and was recognized by them in the breaking of bread. As they spoke, Jesus Himself stood in the midst of them, saying: "Peace be unto you." They were terrified at first, thinking He was a ghost, but He said to them: "See and touch My hands and feet!"

3. "Has a ghost flesh and bones?" And He ate before them a piece of broiled fish and honeycomb. Then He said to them: "As the Father has sent Me, even so I send you." After this, He breathed on them, saying: "Now receive the power of the Holy Spirit."

4. But Thomas was not with them at the time, and when he was told that Jesus had come to them, he did not believe it.

5. "Unless I see and feel the print of the nails in His hands, and thrust my hand into His side, I will not believe," he declared.

6. A week later, Jesus came to them again. He said to Thomas: "Reach out your finger and look at My hands—thrust your hand into My side; and be not faithless, but believing!" Thomas cried: "My Lord, and my God!" "Thomas," said Jesus, "because you have seen Me, you have believed. Blessed are they who have not seen, and yet have believed."

Peter and the risen Lord

1. After this, the disciples went to Galilee. At Tiberias, Peter said: "I am going fishing." Thomas, Nathanael, James and John and two others followed. But they caught nothing all night. As they neared the shore in the morning, they saw One standing there.

2. He called: "Lads, have you anything to eat?" "No!" they shouted back. "Then cast your net over the right side of the ship."

3. They did so, and found it full of fish. John whispered to Peter: "It is the Lord!" Peter tucked his robe into his belt——

4. —and jumped into the water. The others came up in the boat. Fish was laid on a fire, bread ready. "Bring some of the fish you have caught," said Jesus.

5. Peter obeyed Him. Then Jesus invited them to eat. None dared to ask Him Who He was, knowing it was the Lord. Then Jesus gave them the bread and the fish.

6. After they had eaten, Jesus and Peter walked along the sea-shore. "Peter," said Jesus, "do you love Me more than the others?" "Yes, Lord, Thou knowest that I love Thee," said Peter. "Then feed My lambs," said Jesus. Again Jesus asked: "Peter, *do* you love Me?"

7. "Lord, Thou *knowest* that I love Thee!" "Then feed My sheep." Later Jesus asked a third time: "Do you indeed love Me?" Peter cried: "Lord, Thou knowest all——

8. "—Thou knowest that I truly love Thee." "Feed My sheep," Jesus said again; then: "When you are old, you will be carried where you do not want to go."

9. Now John was following them, and Peter, turning round, saw him and asked Jesus: "Lord, what will happen to him?" Jesus checked Peter's curiosity with the reply: "If I want him to wait until I come, what is that to you? Make sure you follow Me yourself."

He appears to many

1. Jesus had made arrangements with His disciples to meet them on a mountain in Galilee. There the eleven gathered with over five hundred of His faithful followers. When they saw Him, they worshipped, though some still doubted. Then Jesus said: "All power is given unto Me in heaven and in earth—go you, therefore, and teach all nations.

2. "Baptize them in the name of the Father and of the Son and of the Holy Ghost, teaching them to observe all things which I have commanded you; and lo, I am with you always, even unto the end of the world."

The Ascension

1. For forty days Jesus had been appearing and as suddenly departing. The disciples knew now that, whether they could see Him or not, He would always be near.

2. Then He came again, and led them out towards Bethany; and there, on the Mount of Olives, He blessed them.

3. He promised them the power and comfort of the Holy Spirit. Then a cloud parted Him from their sight.

4. As they stared at the receding cloud, two men in white stood by them. "Why do you stand gazing up into heaven, you men of Galilee?" they asked. "This same Jesus, Who is taken from you into heaven, will come again, just as you have seen Him go into heaven."

PART II

The Story of His People

JESUS was born among the Jews, in Palestine, nearly two thousand years ago. To understand why, one must know their history. In this section are the stories of His people as His mother must have told them to Him, and the truths His teachers taught, selected from the history of the Jews as we have it in our Old Testament. The section ends with a brief account of their history in the years between the Old Testament and the New. We have not attempted to separate stories which some scholars regard as mere tales told to stress a truth, from stories of actual happenings, nor have we altered the familiar Bible sequence even when there are those who think a particular part of the story belongs to some other time. Here, then, are the stories Jesus loved—of His people and God's dealings with them, and their hopes of a Deliverer ("Messiah" or "Saviour") which He knew Himself to be fulfilling.

Beginning with the Hebrew account of the Creation and man's disobedience, we shall see how God worked through the centuries to bring man back to Himself. First He chose a man, Abraham, with whom He made a "covenant"—called the Old Covenant (so our "Old Testament") to distinguish it from the New Covenant (so our "New Testament") which He made in Jesus. Through Abraham God raised up a family—Jacob, whom He called Israel, and his twelve sons, the fathers of the twelve tribes of Israel. Then He shaped them into a nation, giving them, through Moses, His Law summarized in the Ten Commandments, and bringing them to Palestine, the land He had promised to their forefathers. We shall see how He sent leaders and kings, priests and prophets to guide them, and how again and again they turned from Him and their story became full of defeat and pain and sorrow. Yet God never failed to love them and to purpose that through them the whole of mankind might know and serve Him until the Kingdom of God was in all men's hearts—"on earth as it is in heaven."

The story of

In the beginning God created the heaven and the earth. There was darkness before God said: "Let there be light!" Then there was light; and God divided the light from the darkness calling the light Day and the darkness Night. Thus evening and morning were —the first day. The second day God made the firmament, the over-arching sky, and called it Heaven. Then God said: "Let the dry land appear!" and it was so. He

On the fifth day God created great whales and every living creature that moves in the waters, and every bird, and said: "Be fruitful and multiply." Cattle and creeping things and beasts of the earth appeared on the sixth day. Then to complete His Creation, God said: "Let us make *man* after our likeness, and let him have dominion over all living things on the earth."

the Creation

called the dry land Earth, and the waters Seas. And God said: "Let the Earth bring forth grass, the herb yielding seed and the fruit-trees yielding fruit." That was the third day. On the fourth God made two great lights, the greater light to rule the day and the lesser light to rule the night. He made the stars also, and set them in the heavens. They were to give light upon the earth, and to be for signs and seasons, and for days and years.

So God created man in His own likeness; he created both male and female. And God saw everything that He had made, and it was very good. Thus the heavens and the earth and all that lived in them were completed. And on the seventh day God ended His work, and He blessed the seventh day and made it holy because He had rested from His labors.

The Garden of Eden

1. God formed Man of the dust of the ground, breathed into his nostrils the breath of life, and Man became a living soul.

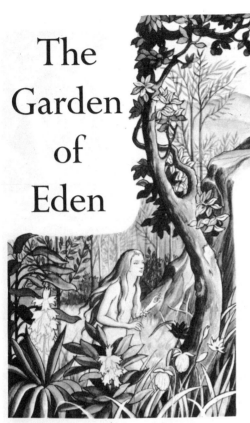

2. God planted a garden eastward in Eden. There He put the man, whom He called Adam. While Adam slept, God took one of his ribs, and made it into a woman.

3. Then Adam said: "This is now bone of my bones and flesh of my flesh; she shall be called Woman." He named the woman Eve, and she became his wife.

4. God said: "The fruit of every tree in the garden you may eat freely, except that of the tree of the knowledge of good and evil, which is in the midst of the garden."

164

5. But the serpent tempted Eve. "If you eat you and Adam shall be as gods——

6. "—knowing good and evil." Then Eve took the fruit, and gave some to Adam.

7. And when they had eaten the fruit, they knew not happiness, but shame and fear; and tried to hide from God. But God knew what he did. He put a curse on the serpent, and promised to send One to overcome the tempter. To Eve, God said: "In sorrow you will bear your children"; to Adam: "Because you have disobeyed Me, the ground is cursed for your sake."

8. "It will grow thorns and thistles. In the sweat of your face you shall eat bread until you return to the ground from which you were taken; for dust you are, and to dust you will return." Then God drove Adam and Eve from Eden, and placed angels with a flaming sword to guard the way to the tree of Life.

Cain and Abel

1. Adam and Eve had two sons, Cain, a farmer, and Abel, who was a shepherd.

2. One day, both brought their offerings to God. God refused Cain's offering because of the sin within his heart; but He accepted Abel's offering.

3. Cain was angry, and killed Abel as they spoke together in a field. Then God called: "Where is Abel, your brother?" "Am I my brother's keeper?" replied Cain.

4. But God cried: "Because of your crime, you shall be an outcast!" "But," cried Cain, "everyone will try to kill me!"

5. But God said: "Not so: vengeance will be taken on the man who kills Cain." And He set a mark on him lest anyone finding him should kill him. Then Cain went to live in the land of Nod, east of Eden.

The Flood

1. The number of men increased on the earth, but God saw that they were wicked. Only one man, Noah, and his family listened to God and obeyed Him. To Noah God said: "I am going to wipe man, whom I created, from the face of the earth. Make an ark for yourself and your family, for I will save you and will make My covenant with you."

2. When Noah had built his ark according to God's commands, he went into it with his wife and his sons, Shem, Ham and Japheth, and their wives. He also took into the ark two (a male and a female) of every living thing. Seven days later, when they were all in, the waters of the flood came upon the earth, for God had said: "I will blot out all I have made."

167

3. The fountains of the great deep were broken up, the windows of heaven opened, and it rained for forty days and nights. Everything died; but the ark was borne upon the face of the waters.

4. After a hundred and fifty days the waters decreased and the ark rested on the mountains of Ararat. Forty days later, Noah released a dove. She could find no resting-place, and returned to the ark.

5. When, a week later, he sent her out and she returned bearing an olive branch, Noah knew that the waters had gone.

6. Then God called upon Noah to bring out his family, and all the living things that had been kept safe in the ark. And when they had come out, Noah built an altar and made an offering. Then God said: "I will not curse the ground any more for man's sake." And He set the rainbow in the sky as a token of His pledge.

168

The Tower of Babel

1. Noah's descendants increased rapidly, but all still spoke the same language.

2. They decided among themselves to make bricks and bake them, and to use slime for mortar; and they began to build a city with a tower, whose top would reach up to heaven.

3. "Let us make a name for ourselves," they said. "We do not want to be scattered abroad over the face of the earth." But God knew that men, in their pride, would——

4. —stop at nothing. So he scattered them, and made them speak different languages. That is why the city, left unfinished, was called Babel—"Confusion."

Abraham, founder of a nation

1. God now chose a man, Abraham, and through him a family and a nation to provide a people in whom the world would be blessed that they might show men what God is like and what He wishes man to do. So Abraham, Sarah his wife——

2. —and Lot, his nephew, journeyed from Mesopotamia to find the Promised Land. But there was a quarrel between their herdsmen and they separated.

3. Abraham went to Canaan. To his sorrow, he and his wife had no children; but one day God promised him an heir, and commanded him to make an offering.

4. God also made a covenant, promising Abraham and his descendants great dominions. When darkness fell, smoking flames were seen on Abraham's offering. Later, there came to him three strangers, messengers from God. Abraham gave them food; and, as they ate, Sarah, at the tent-door, heard the strangers say that she would have a son.

Abraham and Isaac

1. Though Sarah laughed when she heard this, for she was old, God gave her a son, and they called him Isaac. Then, one day, God tested Abraham, saying: "Offer your only son for a burnt offering." So Abraham and Isaac, with two young men, set off for a mountain called Moriah.

2. Leaving the young men at the foot of the mountain, Abraham, with the fire, and Isaac, with the wood, went on. Then Isaac said: "Here are the fire and the wood——

3. "—where is the lamb for the burnt offering?" "My son, God will provide a lamb," said Abraham. Then, when he had built an altar, he bound Isaac.

4. Abraham laid Isaac on the altar, and took up his knife to kill his son. But an angel called to him: "Lay not your hand on the lad; for now I know you fear God, seeing that you would give up your only son!"

5. Then Abraham looked up, and saw that a ram had been caught by its horns in a thicket; and he offered it instead.

Isaac and Rebekah

1. When Abraham was growing old, he sent out his oldest and most trusted servant to the city of his brother Nahor, in Mesopotamia, to seek a wife for Isaac from his own people.

2. At the well outside the city, the servant rested his men and camels. Rebekah, the beautiful grand-daughter of Nahor, came to draw water and gave to them all.

3. When Rebekah's mother and her brother Laban heard how God had guided the servant, they agreed to the marriage, saying: "The Lord has spoken."

4. And Rebekah set off with the servant to be Isaac's wife. Now Isaac, meditating in the fields at eventide, lifted up his eyes and saw the camels coming.

5. He ran to meet them, and, after the servant had told his story, Isaac brought Rebekah to his family. And Rebekah became Isaac's wife.

172

Isaac's twin sons

1. Isaac and Rebekah had twin sons, Esau and Jacob. Esau was a hunter, Jacob a shepherd.

2. Jacob was one day in his tent cooking pottage when Esau came in from the hunt, dying of hunger. He promised his inheritance to Jacob for a bowl of pottage.

3. Years later, when Isaac was old and blind, he begged Esau for a dish of venison, and promised his son his blessing. But Rebekah, while Esau was hunting——

4. —sent in Jacob with venison, covering his neck and hands with goatskins, so that he resembled his hairy brother. Isaac, deceived, gave Jacob Esau's blessing.

5. When Esau came in and heard what had happened, he cried: "He has taken away my birthright, now he has taken away my blessing!" And Esau hated Jacob.

Jacob's vision

Rebekah urged Jacob to flee to her brother Laban, until Esau's anger had died down. Jacob set off. That night, on his journey, he slept out of doors, using a stone for a pillow. And in a dream he saw a stairway stretching from earth to heaven with angels ascending and descending upon it. Above it stood God, saying: "I am the Lord God of Abraham, your father, and the God of Isaac; the land whereon you lie I will give to you and to your children, and they shall spread abroad to the west and to the east, to the north and the south, and in you and them shall all the families of the earth be blessed." Jacob awoke, startled, to find it was dawn. "Surely," he said, "the Lord is in this place, and I knew it not!" And he set up the stone he had used as his pillow, and dedicated it to God; and he called the place Bethel, "The House of God."

Jacob's family

1. So Jacob came to Haran, and there fell in love with Rachel, Laban's daughter, whom he saw for the first time when she brought her father's sheep to be watered.

2. Jacob offered to work for Laban for seven years if he could marry Rachel; but he was tricked into marriage first with her sister, Leah. Jacob's twelve sons——

3. —were the fathers of Israel's twelve tribes: Reuben, Simeon, Levi, Judah, Dan, Naphtali, Gad, Asher, Issacher, Zebulun, Joseph and Benjamin, born long afterwards.

4. God gave Jacob a new name—Israel, "a Prince of God"; his descendants were called Israelites. Remembering God's promise, Jacob returned with his family, servants and cattle to Canaan. When his brother Esau saw him coming, he ran to meet him, embraced him and wept for joy. At Bethel, God repeated His promise, and Jacob built an altar there.

Joseph the dreamer

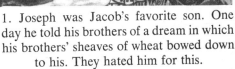

1. Joseph was Jacob's favorite son. One day he told his brothers of a dream in which his brothers' sheaves of wheat bowed down to his. They hated him for this.

3. Now Jacob had given Joseph a coat of many colors; and the brothers dipped it in goat's blood, and brought it to their father.

2. So they decided to kill Joseph. They stripped him, and flung him into a pit in the desert. But when a band of traders passed, the brothers sold him instead.

4. Jacob thought that a wild beast had killed his son and mourned him. But Joseph had been sold as a slave to the captain of Pharaoh's guard, in Egypt.

Joseph in prison

1. Joseph soon found favor in the eyes of his master Potiphar, who made him overseer of all his property.

2. But he aroused the anger of Potiphar's wife.

3. She lied to her husband about him, so Potiphar put him in prison, where were also Pharaoh's butler and baker.

4. One night the butler had a dream in which he squeezed juice from grapes on a three-branched vine into Pharaoh's cup.

5. The same night the baker also had a dream in which he carried three baskets full of good things for Pharaoh; but birds ate all that were in the top basket.

6. Joseph said that the baker's dream meant he would be hanged in three days; the butler's, that he would serve Pharaoh again in three days. And so it was.

177

Ruler in Egypt

1. Two years later Pharaoh was worried by two dreams. In the first, seven fat cows came out of the river, and ate in a meadow; but seven lean cows followed and ate them up. In the second, seven fat ears of corn grew on one stalk, but seven thin ears——

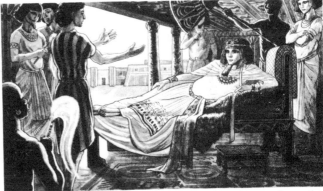

2. —grew after them and, though they were withered and blasted, they ate the fat ears of corn.

3. Then the butler remembered Joseph, who was brought from prison to interpret the dreams. He said: "They mean that seven years of plenty will be followed by seven years of famine."

4. And Joseph advised Pharaoh to appoint a wise man to lay in stocks of corn against the time of famine. "You shall be the man, and rule in Egypt," said Pharaoh.

5. So, during the good years, Joseph stored much corn. When the famine came, he opened the granaries, and all countries came to Egypt to buy corn.

Joseph forgives his brothers

1. Among those who came were Joseph's brothers. They did not recognize him.

2. Then Joseph ordered his brothers to bring to Egypt the youngest, Benjamin, who had stayed at home with Jacob. Simeon he bound and kept with him.

3. But Jacob feared he would lose Benjamin, and would not agree. Then they found that their money had been returned with the corn, and they were afraid.

4. They did not know that Joseph had arranged this. At last they had to go to Egypt to buy again, and took Benjamin with them. Joseph feasted them all—

5. —but he favored Benjamin. Then, on the way home, Joseph's soldiers overtook them and found not only the money, but, in Benjamin's sack, Joseph's silver cup.

179

6. Terrified, the brothers returned to Joseph. Judah offered to stay as a slave in place of Benjamin, saying that if the lad did not go home, it would break his father's heart, for he had already lost one of his sons.

7. No longer could Joseph refrain from making himself known. Ordering everyone, except his brothers, to leave, he cried: "I am Joseph, whom you sold into slavery!" And he and Benjamin embraced, and wept for joy. So Joseph forgave his brothers, and he told them to bring Jacob, their father, and all their families to Egypt.

8. Thus Jacob (or Israel) and his sons came to Egypt with their families and cattle, and went to live in Goshen as shepherds; and Pharaoh welcomed them kindly.

9. But the years passed; Israel, now an old man, died after blessing his twelve sons. The sons died too, and so did the king who knew Joseph. A new Pharaoh ruled.

180

Moses, prince and shepherd

1. The number of the Israelites in Egypt grew, and, fearing them, the Egyptians forced them into slavery. When they still flourished the order went forth: "Every boy that is born is to be drowned." But one Hebrew woman saved her child.

2. She made him an ark of bulrushes, and hid him in the flags of the river's bank. There he was found by Pharaoh's daughter and called Moses.

3. When he was grown up, Moses one day killed an Egyptian who had beaten a Hebrew, then fled to Midian. While he was living as a shepherd, he had a vision.

4. God spoke to him from a burning bush, called on him to lead the Israelites out of Egypt, and promised that they should find a rich land. Aaron was to be his spokesman.

5. Then God gave Moses a staff. He returned to Egypt, and called the Israelites together; and Aaron told them of God's promise to free them from the Egyptians.

The Passover

1. But Pharaoh refused to let the Israelites go, in spite of nine terrible plagues sent by God. So Moses commanded the Israelites to make a sacrifice—a lamb for each house.

2. They dipped a bunch of herbs in the blood and marked their doorposts with it. Then, ready for travel, they ate the roasted lamb with unleavened bread.

3. At midnight a great cry went up in Egypt, for the firstborn of all the Egyptians and of all their cattle died. But this disaster passed over the Israelites.

4. At once Pharaoh and all the Egyptians begged the Israelites to leave their land, giving them jewels and silver. So the Israelites went with their cattle and flocks. And God ordered that the night of the Passover and the departure should always be remembered.

The Red Sea

1. The Israelites journeyed towards the Red Sea; before them went a pillar of cloud by day and a pillar of fire by night, to guide them. By the Red Sea they encamped.

2. But Pharaoh, who regretted letting the Israelites go, pursued them with an army of horsemen and chariots. When they saw the Egyptians, the people were afraid.

3. In answer to their cries, God told Moses to stretch out his staff over the sea, and the waters were divided by a strong east wind, making it possible to cross on land.

4. All the Israelites marched over safely. But when Pharaoh's chariots pursued them, the wheels quickly became bogged.

5. Once again Moses stretched out his staff over the waters; and they came together and swept over the Egyptians.

God gives Moses the

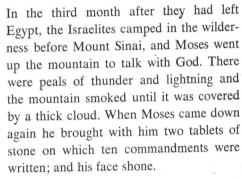

In the third month after they had left Egypt, the Israelites camped in the wilderness before Mount Sinai, and Moses went up the mountain to talk with God. There were peals of thunder and lightning and the mountain smoked until it was covered by a thick cloud. When Moses came down again he brought with him two tablets of stone on which ten commandments were written; and his face shone.

These are the Ten Commandments which God gave Moses to guide the lives of His people:

And God spake all these words, saying: "I am the Lord thy God, which have brought thee out of the land of Egypt, out of the house of bondage.

1. *Thou shalt have no other gods before me.*

2. *Thou shalt not make unto thee any graven image, or any likeness of any thing that is in heaven above, or that is in the earth beneath, or that is in the water under the earth: Thou shalt not bow down thyself to them, nor serve them: for I the Lord thy God am a jealous God visiting the iniquity of the fathers upon the children unto the third and fourth generation of them that hate Me; and shewing mercy unto thousands of them that love Me and keep My commandments.*

Ten Commandments

3. *Thou shalt not take the name of the Lord thy God in vain; for the Lord will not hold him guiltless that taketh His name in vain.*

4. *Remember the sabbath day to keep it holy. Six days shalt thou labor and do all thy work; but the seventh day is the sabbath of the Lord thy God; in it thou shalt not do any work, thou, nor thy son, nor thy daughter, nor thy manservant, nor thy maidservant, nor thy cattle, nor thy stranger that is within thy gates: for in six days the Lord made heaven and earth, the sea, and all that in them is, and rested the seventh day: wherefore the Lord blessed the sabbath day, and hallowed it.*

5. *Honor thy father and thy mother: that thy days may be long upon the land which the Lord thy God giveth thee.*

6. *Thou shalt not kill.*

7. *Thou shalt not commit adultery.*

8. *Thou shalt not steal.*

9. *Thou shalt not bear false witness against thy neighbor.*

10. *Thou shalt not covet thy neighbor's house, thou shalt not covet thy neighbor's wife, nor his manservant, nor his maidservant, nor his ox, nor his ass, nor any thing that is thy neighbor's."*

The land of milk and honey

1. Spies sent to the Promised Land brought back clusters of grapes which had to be carried by two men.

2. "It is a land flowing with milk and honey," they said, telling of its wonders. "But the cities are walled, and the people are giants and stronger than we."

3. The disappointed Israelites wept, and would have stoned Joshua and Caleb, two of the spies who urged them to trust in the Lord. Suddenly, a great light––

4. –shone in the Tent of Meeting. Moses and Aaron heard God: "Because you doubted, you shall fall in the wilderness: only your children shall know the Land."

5. So, for forty years, the people wandered in the wilderness. And within sight of the borders of the Promised Land, Aaron gave up his priestly robes to his son, and died.

Balaam's ass

1. The Israelites now marched into the country east of Jordan and won great victories. So Balak, King of Moab, called on Balaam, a famous prophet, to curse the Israelites in God's name. At first he refused to do so.

2. But a second deputation of Moabite princes persuaded him. On his way to the King, his ass saw an angel, and fell down under him. Balaam beat her angrily.

3. Then Balaam, too, saw the angel with a drawn sword, and bowed down. "Go with the princes," said the angel; "but when you speak, you shall speak only God's word."

4. When Balaam came to Balak, the King took him to a high place overlooking the Israelites' camp. Balaam called for seven altars and sacrifices to be made.

5. But when called upon to curse the Israelites, Balaam could only bless them, saying: "There cometh a Star out of Israel. He shall have dominion."

187

The fall of Jericho

1. The Israelites eventually defeated the Midianites, and Moses appointed Joshua to take his place. After blessing the people he climbed Mount Nebo, overlooking the Promised Land, and there he died.

2. Joshua sent spies over the Jordan to Jericho. Rahab, a woman whose house was on the city wall, sheltered them, letting them down by a rope through her window.

3. Next day, the priests bore the Ark before the army to the Jordan, and the waters parted so that the host crossed on dry land.

4. And as a memorial, twelve great stones from the Jordan bed were set up. Then the Israelites ate their first Passover in the Promised Land.

5. As Joshua was planning his campaign, a vision appeared to him of a man with his sword drawn in his hand, who said he was "Captain of the army of the Lord." He outlined the campaign to Joshua.

6. And, as he had said, when all the Israelites had marched round Jericho once each day for six days, with the Ark and seven priests, each blowing a ram's horn, leading them; and on the seventh day seven times, ending with a great blast, and all shouting, the walls of Jericho fell. Then they completely destroyed the city.

The conquering host

1. Having secured the passes with the central hills of Palestine, Joshua sent a small army to take the city of Ai, but it was defeated and fled.

2. And Joshua and the elders of Israel asked God the cause of their downfall, and why He had brought them over the Jordan only for them to be destroyed.

3. Then God told Joshua that one of the Israelites had disobeyed Him and hidden some of the spoils taken at Jericho. Gold and silver were found in Achan's tent.

4. Joshua dealt with him severely. Then he attacked Ai again, feigning flight with his forces on the front, while forces from the back of the city entered and set fire to it as the men of Ai were pursuing the "fleeing" Israelites.

5. After this victory Joshua raised an altar of stones on Mount Ebal, inscribing them, after sacrifice, with the ten commandments.

6. The Israelites were tricked into alliance with the men of Gibeon. At once five southern princes massed armies against the city.

7. In answer to the Gibeonites' call for help, the Israelites made a forced march and routed the enemy. A great hailstorm killed many more as they fled.

8. After victory in the south, the Israelites had to meet the combined armies of the northern princes. Joshua fell upon them by the waters of Merom.

9. The Canaanite armies, with their horses and chariots, were defeated; and Hazor, their capital city, was burned.

10. The ageing Joshua, reminding the tribes of God's Covenant, set up a pillar bearing its words. Shortly afterwards he died.

Death of a tyrant

1. Some years later the Canaanites, under Jabin, and led by his captain Sisera, swept over Palestine with many chariots and archers, and for long the Israelites were a subject people. Then Deborah, a prophetess, called Barak to her house and prophesied deliverance if he would go to Mount Tabor with ten thousand men.

2. "If you will go with me, then will I go," answered Barak; and so Deborah went with Barak at the head of the Israelites. They swooped from the mountainside on the forces of Sisera by the brook Kishon just as a storm began. The stream was flooded, the enemy archers were blinded with rain, and their chariots were bogged or swept away.

3. Sisera fled on foot and sought refuge in the tent of Jael whom he thought friendly; and indeed she pretended to be so.

4. When he asked for water, she gave him milk. But as he slept, she drove a nail through his head. Thus was Israel delivered.

Gideon saves Israel

1. After forty years of peace, the Midianites began killing and plundering the Israelites. But an angel of the Lord appeared to Gideon, and said: "You shall save Israel." As a sign, the angel touched his offering of goat's flesh and bread, and flames burst from them.

2. Again, when Gideon put a fleece on the ground, it was wet with dew when the ground was dry——

3. —and dry when the ground was wet. Then he rallied to him men from all Israel. From these he chose three hundred —the most watchful and reliable. To each of them he gave a trumpet, a pitcher and a torch; and at dead of night——

4. —they surrounded the enemy camp. At Gideon's signal, the trumpets blared, the pitchers crashed, the torches blazed, and the cry arose: "The sword of the Lord and of Gideon!" The enemy, suddenly awakened, fled in panic over the River Jordan.

Jephthah's daughter

1. Later, the Ammonites attacked Israel; and the elders went to beg Jephthah (who, on being thrown out of his home, had become an outlaw chief) to lead the Israelite army.

2. They promised that they would make him their chief. Before the battle Jephthah vowed that, if victorious, he would sacrifice whatever first met him on his return.

3. And he won great victories against the Ammonites. But as he returned to his house, his daughter, his only child, came to meet him with music and dancing.

4. Then Jephthah rent his clothes and despairingly told her of the vow he had made. She replied: "My father, you must do what you have promised. God has given you victory." And year by year, the women of Israel remembered with mourning her courage.

The story of Samson

1. Samson was a young Israelite who had a giant's strength. One day he met a lion and killed it with his bare hands.

2. Returning later, he found that bees had made honey in the lion's corpse. And so he made a riddle, and asked it at his wedding feast: "Out of the eater came forth meat; and out of the strong came forth sweetness." His Philistine guests could not solve it, but his Philistine wife wheedled the answer from him and told them. Later, she married another man.

3. In revenge, Samson destroyed the Philistines' harvest. So the Philistines made war on Judah. The Jews bound Samson——

4. —to hand him over to the Philistines, but he snapped the cords. Then, with an ass's jawbone, he slew a thousand Philistines.

195

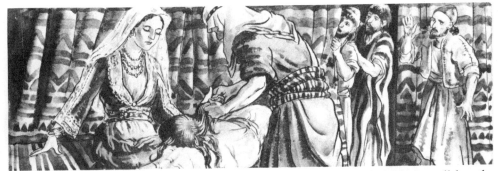

5. Samson loved another Philistine woman, Delilah. She persuaded him to tell her the secret of his strength. It was that, before he was born, his mother devoted him to God as a Nazarite, which meant that his hair had never been cut. So while he slept, Delilah had his head shaved. And the Philistines took him, bound him, and put out his eyes.

6. But while he was in prison his hair began to grow again. Then the Philistines held a feast in the temple of their god, Dagon, and brought out Samson to mock him. Samson asked the lad who led him to put his hands on the central pillars of the temple. Suddenly, putting out all his strength, he cracked the pillars; and the temple fell, killing him with them.

196

Ruth

1. There was a famine in Palestine, and a man called Elimelech went with his wife, Naomi, into Moab. There his two sons married Moabite women——

2. —whose names were Orpah and Ruth. But the father and the sons died; and hearing that there was food again at home, Naomi decided to return. Orpah kissed her farewell; but Ruth said: "Where you go, I will go; where you stay, I will stay; your people shall be my people, and your God, my God."

3. So they came to Bethlehem at harvesttime. Ruth went out to glean, picking up the corn left by the reapers. The owner of the field, Boaz, saw and fell in love with her.

4. Because he was a relative of Elimelech, he bought back Elimelech's land for Naomi. Then he married Ruth. Their son, Obed, was the grandfather of David.

197

Samuel the prophet

1. Hannah, wife of Elkanah of Ramathaim-zophim, went to the temple at Shiloh and promised Eli the priest that if God would send her a son she would give him to the Lord.

2. God answered her prayers, and Hannah, according to her promise, brought her son Samuel, when he was still a child, to Eli, to serve God in the temple.

3. One night, as Samuel lay asleep, God called him. Samuel answered: "Here I am," and ran to Eli, thinking the priest had called him.

4. "I did not call you," said Eli. "Sleep again." Three times Samuel was called, and at last Eli realized that God wished to speak to the boy.

5. The fourth time Samuel answered: "Speak, Lord, for Thy servant heareth." Then God told him of judgment to fall on Eli's evil sons.

6. Samuel later became a prophet. When Eli was very old he sent his sons into battle.

7. There they perished, and the Ark they had taken was captured by the Philistines.

8. The Philistines placed the Ark in the temple of their god Dagon, at Ashdod. Next day they found the image of Dagon fallen, face downwards, before the Ark. They set the image up again; but when they came back next morning it had again fallen. This time the head and hands were broken off.

9. So they returned the Ark. Then the Israelites, who had taken to worshipping idols, confessed their sinfulness and went to battle against the Philistines.

10. Samuel prayed for the Israelites and they won a great victory at Mizpah. There Samuel erected a memorial stone and called it Ebenezer, "the stone of help."

Saul is chosen king

1. When Samuel was old, the elders of Israel said: "Give us a king to rule us and to go out before us and fight our battles."

2. Now Saul, the son of Kish, was searching with a servant for his father's lost asses, and learning there was a seer in the town he went to Samuel for help.

3. The Lord had told Samuel how to recognize the man to be king; and the next day Samuel took Saul aside and anointed him in the Lord's name.

4. When Samuel called the people to Mizpah, and showed to them Saul, who stood head and shoulders above them, they shouted: "God save the King!"

5. Saul was made king at Gilgal. Then he summoned the people to fight the Philistines. But when they saw the enemy host, they hid in caves among the mountains.

Jonathan and the Philistines

1. Jonathan, the son of Saul, looked across the valley to the Philistines' camp, and said to his armor bearer: "Come, let us go over; for the Lord can save by many or by few."

2. So they showed themselves to the Philistine guards and challenged them. "Come up," said the guards, "and we will show you a thing!"

3. So Jonathan climbed up to the garrison on his hands and feet, and threw down guard after guard, and his armor bearer slew them behind him.

4. The slaughter created a panic in the Philistine camp, which a sudden earthquake increased, making the Philistines fight one another and flee.

5. Then Saul gathered the Israelites together out of their hiding-places and pursued the Philistines. There was that day a great victory.

David
the shepherd

1. But Saul became too proud and disobeyed God; and Samuel told him that the Lord would reject him.

2. And God sent Samuel to Bethlehem to choose a king from among the sons of a man called Jesse. Seven sons passed before Samuel; then he asked Jesse if there were any others. "Only the youngest, looking after the sheep." "Send and fetch him," said Samuel. So David, a red-haired and handsome youth, came to him.

3. And Samuel, in the presence of David's brothers, anointed him, for the Lord had said: "This is he."

4. From that time the Spirit of the Lord was upon David. Saul was now troubled with fits of madness, and David, who was a skilled musician, was chosen to play the harp to the King to calm him at such times.

David and Goliath

1. Now the champion of the Philistines was a giant named Goliath, who challenged Israel. When David heard of this——

2. —he offered to fight Goliath. "You are too young," said Saul. But David told him he had slain a lion and a bear which had attacked his father's sheep.

3. So, with Saul's blessing, David went forth to fight. From a brook he chose five smooth stones, which he put in the shepherd's bag he carried; and he took his sling.

4. When Goliath saw David, he sneered at his youth and cursed him. But David defied him, and taking a stone slung it straight at the Philistine.

5. The stone sank into Goliath's forehead and he fell face downwards. Then David ran, drew Goliath's sword from its sheath, and slew and beheaded the giant.

Saul's jealousy

1. Because of David's triumph in the Philistine wars, the women from the cities of Israel met him, singing: "Saul has slain his thousands, but David his ten thousands."

2. Saul became very jealous of David; and when David played to the King next day, Saul cast his javelin at him. But David escaped. Then, because David behaved wisely, Saul feared him.

3. Later, David and his men slew two hundred Philistines to win Michal, Saul's daughter, as his wife. But Saul sought to kill him.

4. Saul's son, Jonathan, loved David, gave him his own possessions, and tried to turn his father's anger away. David escaped when Saul again threw his javelin——

5. —and fled to his home; but Saul sent messengers to watch and kill him. Then Michal helped him to get away, and placed an image in the bed to foil them.

6. Jonathan failed to make peace, and by an arrow signal warned David against Saul.

7. So David fled to the cave of Adullam as chief to four hundred outlawed men.

8. Saul surrounded David and his men, but was recalled to fight the Philistines. He returned with three thousand men, but went to sleep in the very cave where David and his men were hiding. David spared Saul's life, cutting off a piece from the King's robe. Afterwards, he showed it to Saul. "The Lord will reward you," said Saul. "I know you will be king."

9. On yet another occasion David spared Saul's life. He called across the valley, showing Saul a spear and water-bottle he had stolen from his camp.

10. But David knew Saul would kill him if he could, so he joined forces with King Achish, a Philistine. Achish went out to fight against Saul.

205

The death of Saul

1. Samuel had died, and Saul, fearing the Philistines, went in disguise to a witch at Endor.

2. When he asked her to bring up Samuel's spirit, she recognized Saul. Samuel's message was that Saul and his sons would die, and the kingdom pass to David.

3. Meanwhile, the Philistine princes mistrusted David, for they feared he would turn against them in battle for Saul's sake. So King Achish had to send David away.

4. There was a fierce battle between the Philistines and Israelites, and Jonathan and two of his brothers were killed on Mount Gilboa.

5. The Philistine archers also wounded Saul so badly that, not wishing to fall into his enemy's hands, he killed himself with his own sword.

The capture of Jerusalem

1. After Saul's death David was anointed King of the House of Judah at Hebron.

2. But Abner, Saul's general, had Ish-bosheth, Saul's son, crowned King of Israel. Then men of Judah fought men of Israel at Gibeon; and the Israelites were beaten.

3. Abner called for a treaty, and David agreed. But Abner was slain by Joab to avenge his brother's death at Gibeon.

4. At last all the tribes of Israel agreed to have David as their king, and he made a treaty with them when they came to him at Hebron.

5. But Jerusalem was not yet David's, and the city defied him until Joab gained an entry into the city by a water-tunnel. Then David took the stronghold of Zion, and made the city his capital.

King David

1. And David, in celebration of his victories, brought the Ark to Jerusalem, which became known as "the city of David," and led the joyous procession, dancing before the Ark. And David built a palace for himself, and would have built a temple to the Lord, to house the Ark, but the prophet Nathan told him that God had destined this work for his son.

2. Later, David married Bathsheba, widow of Uriah the Hittite. Their son was eventually to become the wise King Solomon.

3. David reigned over Israel for forty years, subduing the surrounding nations, increasing the kingdom and fearing God. He was the greatest king in the history of Israel.

"The Lord is my Shepherd"

No picture of the Bible would be complete without some account of its poetry, and, in particular, the Book of Psalms. Though written so long ago, they have expressed the deepest thoughts and emotions of men all over the world, and in every generation.

Here is the best known of them all—said to have been written by David himself—Psalm xxiii; "God is to His people as a shepherd to his flock."

The Lord is my Shepherd; I shall not want.

He maketh me to lie down in green pastures: He leadeth me beside the still waters.

He restoreth my soul: He leadeth me in the paths of righteousness for His name's sake.

Yea, though I walk through the valley of the shadow of death, I will fear no evil: for Thou art with me; Thy rod and Thy staff they comfort me.

Thou preparest a table before me in the presence of mine enemies: Thou anointest my head with oil; my cup runneth over.

Surely goodness and mercy shall follow me all the days of my life: and I will dwell in the house of the Lord for ever.

"I will lift up mine eyes"

Psalm cxxi is the song of the traveller who looks up to the hills and remembers their dangers; but also recalls that his Guide and Guard is "The Lord, Who made heaven and earth."

I will lift up mine eyes unto the hills. From whence cometh my help?

My help cometh from the Lord, which made heaven and earth.

He will not suffer thy foot to be moved: He that keepeth thee will not slumber.

Behold, He that keepeth Israel shall neither slumber nor sleep.

The Lord is thy Keeper; the Lord is thy shade upon thy right hand.

The sun shall not smite thee by day, nor the moon by night.

The Lord shall preserve thee from all evil: He shall preserve thy soul.

The Lord shall preserve thy going out and thy coming in from this time forth, and even for evermore.

The reign of Solomon

1. When he was old, David recognized Solomon as king in preference to Adonijah, another son.

2. So Solomon reigned in David's stead when the old king died. Now Solomon loved God as his father had done, and determined to build a Temple to the Lord. He called for the help of Hiram, King of Tyre, and a Temple was erected, into the holiest place of which, the "Holy of Holies," the Ark was brought. He also built palaces for himself.

3. The Queen of Sheba heard of Solomon's wisdom and greatness, and came to Jerusalem with a great company and much treasure. She also saw his wealth, and heard his wise answers to her questions; then praised him, saying: "Happy are your servants, who continually hear your wisdom." At the same time she presented him with gifts of gold, jewels and spices.

4. Solomon had asked God: "Give Thy servant an understanding heart." How truly God answered his prayer was shown when two women came before him with a baby, each claiming it as her own, and asking him to decide whose the child was. "Divide it and give half to each!" he commanded; and immediately gave it to the mother who cried out: "No!"

Proverbs

*Following the Book of Psalms come The Proverbs.
It is a collection of pithy sayings, similar to our
proverbs, but it is more—it is a guide to daily life.
The sayings are concerned with wisdom. Wisdom,
they say, is the art of living well; and therefore there
is no true wisdom apart from faith in God. "The
fear of the Lord is the beginning of wisdom."*

The Proverbs were written to give the young
man knowledge and discretion . . .

Wisdom crieth: "Unto you, O men, I call: and
my voice is to the sons of men.

"O ye simple, understand wisdom, for wisdom
is better than rubies; and all the things that may be
desired are not to be compared to it.

"By me kings reign, and princes decree justice.

"I love them that love me: and those that seek
me early shall find me. Riches and honor are
with me; yea, durable riches and righteousness.

"The Lord possessed me in the beginning of His
way, while as yet He had not made the earth.

"Blessed is the man that heareth me, watching
daily at my gates; for whoso findeth me findeth life.

"The fear of the Lord is the beginning of wisdom;
and the knowledge of the holy is understanding."

Wise sayings

There are many more proverbs.

Here are some that lay stress on the simple virtues of character, honesty and loving helpfulness in everyday life; and which emphasize that faith in God is more important than any other thing in the search for wise and selfless living.

A soft answer turneth away wrath: but grievous words stir up anger.

Better is little with the fear of the Lord than great treasure and trouble therewith. Better is a dinner of herbs where love is, than a stalled ox and hatred therewith.

Children's children are the crown of old men; and the glory of children are their fathers.

A good name is rather to be chosen than great riches, and loving favor rather than silver and gold.

Two things have I required of Thee: deny me them not before I die:

Remove far from me vanity and lies: give me neither poverty nor riches; feed me with food convenient for me: lest I be full and deny Thee, and say, "Who is the Lord?" or lest I be poor, and steal, and take the name of my God in vain.

Who can find a virtuous woman? for her price is far above rubies. She seeketh wool, and flax, and worketh willingly with her hands. Strength and honor are her clothing. She looketh well to the ways of her household. Her children arise up and call her blessed: her husband also, and he praiseth her.

Rival kingdoms

1. Solomon's magnificent buildings had laid a heavy burden in taxes and labor on the people; and when his son, Rehoboam, became king, Jeroboam, for the people, asked for their burden to be lightened.

2. But Rehoboam threatened to make it heavier, taking the advice of his young companions rather than that of his older and wiser counsellors.

3. So Jeroboam led a rebellion. He was crowned king over the ten tribes of Israel in the north.

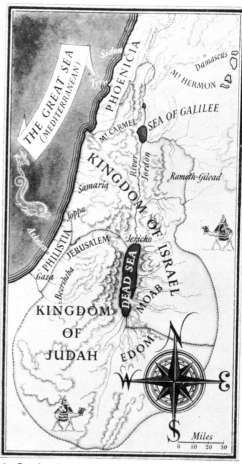

4. In the South, Rehoboam ruled over the two remaining tribes, Judah and Benjamin, with his kingdom centering on Jerusalem.

215

Elijah the prophet

1. Because they worshipped Baal, Elijah warned Ahab, King of Israel, and Jezebel, his wife——

2. —that there would be a three-year drought. Then he hid himself, but was fed, morning and evening, by ravens.

3. At last God ordered him to leave his hiding-place by the brook, Cherith, and go to Zarephath, where a poor widow lived. When he asked for food, she was about to make her last meal.

4. But first she fed Elijah, and while he lodged at her house she never wanted. When her son fell ill and died, Elijah laid the child on his own bed, and cried to God:

5. "Let the child live!" God restored his life, and Elijah brought him to his mother.

Jehovah or Baal

1. At the end of the three years of drought, King Ahab and the controller of his household were seeking pasture for the cattle. They met Elijah, and Ahab asked: "Have you brought this trouble on Israel?"

2. "Not I, but you and your people who worship Baal," said Elijah. Then he told Ahab to summon the priests of Baal and the Israelites to Mount Carmel. There two bullocks were placed on altars. The priests of Baal called frenziedly on their god to bring down fire. It did not come, and Elijah mocked their efforts.

3. Then Elijah ordered that barrels of water should three times be poured over the wood and the sacrifice on the altar of Jehovah; and the trench, which he had dug around the altar, was filled with water. And he prayed: "Lord, show that Thou art God in Israel."

4. And the fire of the Lord fell and consumed not only the sacrifice on the altar, but the wood, the stones and the dust, and licked up the water in the trench. When the people saw it they fell on their faces, and cried: "Jehovah! He is God!" And all the priests of Baal were captured by the people and killed.

5. Then Elijah sent his servant to look towards the sea. He saw a small cloud arising. So Ahab rode in his chariot to Jezreel, and Elijah ran before the King to the gates of the city. Meanwhile, the skies were black with clouds and wind, and there was a great rain.

The still, small voice

1. When Queen Jezebel heard how the priests of Baal had been slain, she sent word to Elijah, threatening to have him killed. So he fled. Again he was miraculously fed, and on the strength of that food he made his way to a cave on Mount Horeb.

2. "What are you doing here, Elijah?" God said to him. "I, even I only, am left of Thy prophets; and they seek to kill me," he complained. Then the Lord commanded him to stand on the mountain and see God passing by; and a great wind broke the rocks in pieces. There was an earthquake, and after that fire.

3. Yet the Lord was not in the wind, nor the earthquake, nor the fire; but after the fire there was a still, small voice.

4. Hearing it, Elijah covered his face. And God told Elijah: "I have still left in Israel seven thousand faithful to My name."

The calling of Elisha

1. Leaving Mount Horeb, Elijah found Elisha, who was ploughing, and cast his mantle over him.

2. Elisha became Elijah's constant attendant. Some years later, a group of prophets in Jericho told him: "The Lord will take away your master today."

3. So Elisha would not leave Elijah. When they came to the Jordan, Elijah struck the waters with his mantle. They divided, and the two crossed on dry land.

4. As they were speaking together, a chariot and horses of fire parted them, and Elijah was carried up to heaven by a whirlwind; and his mantle fell to Elisha.

Stories of Elisha

1. With Elijah's mantle, Elisha inherited his powers as a prophet. One day a widow, in debt, told him her sons were to be sold as slaves, and begged his help. "What have you in your house?" Elisha asked. "Only one pot of oil," she said.

2. Elisha told her to borrow empty jars from neighbors, and from her one pot to fill them all. She did so, and then sold the oil to pay her debts.

3. A rich woman, in whose house Elisha lived, had a son. One day he joined his father, reaping in the fields. Suddenly the child cried: "My head, my head!"

4. Later that day he died. But Elisha restored him to life and brought him back to his joyful mother.

5. Another time, as the prophet was sitting with a hundred companions, all the food he had was twenty barley loaves. "Set them before them—it will be enough for all," said Elisha to his servant. And so it was.

Naaman the leper

1. Elisha's fame spread to Syria. There Naaman, captain of the King's army, was a leper. His wife's maid, an Israelite girl captured by the Syrians, said to her mistress: "Would that my lord were with the prophet who lives in Samaria!

2. "He would heal his leprosy." So the King of Syria sent Naaman to the King of Israel for his recovery. The King of Israel feared that the King of Syria wanted an excuse for a quarrel, but Elisha sent word that Naaman should come to him, saying: "Let him come to me, and he shall know that there is a prophet in Israel." So Naaman went forth.

3. He stood with his horses and chariot outside Elisha's door. Elisha sent a messenger, who told Naaman to bathe seven times in the River Jordan, and he would be cured. Angrily Naaman turned away, saying: "Are not Abana and Pharpar, rivers of Damascus, better than all the waters of Israel?"

4. But his servants persuaded him to obey Elisha, saying: "If the prophet had ordered you to do some great thing, surely you would have done it?" So Naaman went down and bathed himself seven times in the River Jordan; and when he came out again his flesh was like that of a child, and he was cured of his leprosy.

5. Then Naaman and all his attendants came to the prophet Elisha, and the Syrian captain said: "Now I know there is no God in all the earth but in Israel." And Naaman asked Elisha to accept gifts from him, but Elisha refused. So Naaman went away, swearing to sacrifice to no other god.

Elisha's chariots of fire

1. Each time the Syrians invaded Israel, Elisha warned King Jehoram of their ambushes.

2. So the Syrians encircled Dothan, where Elisha was. His servant was fearful, but as Elisha prayed he saw that the mountain was full of horses and chariots of fire.

3. Again Elisha prayed, and the Syrians were struck blind. Then he led them to King Jehoram, but forbade him to kill them. Later, they laid siege to Samaria.

4. There was a famine in the city, so Jehoram hurried to Elisha, who prophesied that before evening there would be food.

5. And that day four lepers went to the Syrian camp, and found the enemy had fled, leaving their stores and wealth behind.

Jehu, King of Israel

1. Elisha now sent a prophet to anoint Jehu King over Israel. When this was done, Jehu told his friends and, rejoicing, they followed him to Jezreel, where King Jehoram was recovering from wounds. The watchman on the tower sent him an urgent message:

2. "A company of men is approaching swiftly!" Jehoram sent messengers to ask: "Is it peace?" But they did not return. Again the watchman reported to Jehoram:

3. "The driving is like the furious driving of Jehu!" So Jehoram went to meet Jehu, calling: "Is it peace?" "What peace is there while your mother's witchcraft remains?"

4. Then Jehoram turned to flee, but Jehu shot him through the heart, and entered the city. Jezebel, the King's mother——

5. —called to him from a window. "Who is on my side?" cried Jehu. Her servants threw her down, and she died.

The boy-king of Judah

1. King Ahaziah of Judah, who had been visiting Jehoram, tried to escape from Jehu, but was caught and killed. His mother, Athaliah, a worshipper of Baal, took the throne.

2. She killed Ahaziah's sons, except the baby Joash, who was saved by his aunt, Jehosheba, and hidden in the Temple by the high-priest, Jehoiada.

3. When Joash was seven, Jehoiada placed guards round the Temple; then he showed the people the King's son and crowned him king. They all cheered.

4. Athaliah heard the shouts of "God save the King!" from the guards and the people, and ran to the Temple. When she saw the young king, she cried: "Treason!" But Jehoiada ordered the soldiers to take her out and put her to death.

A king and his arrows

1. In Israel, Elisha, old and dying, sent for King Jehoash, Jehu's grandson, who wept when he saw him so ill.

2. But Elisha raised himself. "Take bow and arrows," he told the King; and he put his own hands on those of the King upon the bow. "Now open the window eastward."

3. When this was done, Elisha commanded him: "Shoot!" Jehoash did so. "That arrow," said Elisha, "is the arrow of the Lord's deliverance from the Syrians!"

4. "Take the arrows and strike the ground!" Jehoash hit the ground three times, then stopped. Elisha was angry. "You should have done it five or six times," he said. "You *will* strike the Syrians, but now only three times." Shortly afterwards Elisha died.

227

The prophet Amos

1. When Jeroboam II, the son of Jehoash, was King of Israel, God called Amos, a shepherd of Tekoa, to proclaim his judgment on Israel.

2. None could escape the justice of God, the prophet proclaimed—neither Israel nor her seven neighbor nations. The wickedness of Samaria would shock even the Egyptians. He named their evils: "They sell the poor for a pair of shoes, stretch themselves on ivory couches, drink wine, sing, and put off the evil day.

3. "But they shall go captive!" he cried. Even so the prophet did not deny all hope. "The day of the Lord, for which some long, will be a day of judgment; but the captivity is a sifting of the seed, and later the good will return from exile."

Hosea

1. At the same time as Amos there was in northern Israel a prophet named Hosea. He lived happily with his family. Gomer, his wife, he loved dearly.

2. "Just as dearly," Hosea told his people, "God loves Israel." But Gomer ran away from her husband. Hosea, heartbroken, searched everywhere for her.

3. Finally, he had to buy her back from slavery. Israel, too, as the prophet saw and said, had left God, forgotten Him, and "joined herself to idols."

4. Yet God loved her and would bring her back to Himself. But first, as with Gomer, she must be shut up for a time by herself.

5. Israel, for her sins, must go into captivity, but God had said: "I will heal their backsliding; I will love them freely."

229

Israel's captivity

1. Ten years later Pekah, King of Israel, and Rezin, King of Syria, at the head of their armies, marched into Judah, and laid siege to Jerusalem.

2. Ahaz, King of Judah, in spite of the protests of Isaiah, sent for help from Tiglath-Pileser, monarch of the great Assyrian empire.

3. He came, destroyed Damascus, killed Rezin, and took some of Israel's cities. But Ahaz was forced to give him the Temple treasure, and do him homage at Damascus.

4. When Hoshea followed Pekah as king, Shalmaneser, successor to Tiglath-Pileser, laid siege to Samaria, capital of Israel. Sargon, emperor after Shalmaneser, destroyed the city in 722 B.C., and scattered the people all over the empire as his captives.

The vision of Isaiah

1. Amos and Hosea spoke to Israel in the north; the south had its prophet, too—Isaiah —and he spoke to Judah. "In the year that King Uzziah died," he wrote, "I saw the Lord.

2. "He sat upon a throne on high; above it were the six-winged seraphim; and one cried to another: 'Holy, Holy, Holy is the Lord of Hosts; the whole earth is full of His glory!' The foundations were shaken by his voice, and the Temple was filled with smoke."

3. "Then said I: 'Woe is me! For I am undone; because I am a man of unclean lips, and I dwell in the midst of a people of unclean lips; for mine eyes have seen the Lord!'

4. "Then flew one of the seraphim unto me, having a glowing coal in his hand which he had taken with the tongs from off the altar; and he laid it upon my mouth saying: 'Lo, this has touched your lips; your iniquity is taken away, and your sin purged.' At the same time I heard the voice of God, saying:

5. " 'Whom shall I send, and who will go for us?' And I answered: 'Here am I; send me.' Then God uttered a warning of the disaster that should come; but He promised that a remnant of the people should be saved."

The prophecy of Isaiah

1. So Isaiah warned the people of Judah: "Because you hear, but will not listen to God's words, a day is coming when you will be removed far away."

2. Later, when Ahaz was King, Israel and Syria joined forces to threaten Judah. Isaiah said to the King: "Fear not; they shall be taken away by Assyria."

3. Twenty years passed, and Hezekiah came to the throne. He put down idol worship, cleansed the Temple, and celebrated the Feast of the Passover.

4. But he refused to pay tribute to Assyria. So the Assyrian king, Sennacherib, sent his officer, Rab-shakeh, with a large force against Jerusalem. "Do you trust in God?" shouted Rab-shakeh. "Where are the gods of other nations conquered by Assyria?"

5. King Hezekiah was greatly troubled, but Isaiah prophesied Sennacherib's death.

6. Sennacherib sent Hezekiah a message, threatening the destruction of his land.

7. Hezekiah prayed in the Temple, and Isaiah promised that God would save Jerusalem. And when the Assyrians besieged the city, a terrible disease spread through the camp overnight, killing thousands of men. So Sennacherib left, and returned to Assyria. There two of his sons killed him while he was at worship.

8. Hezekiah fell ill and the King of Babylon sent him a letter and gifts. So Hezekiah showed the envoys all the rich treasures of Judah.

9. When Isaiah heard this, he said: "Hear the word of God: 'Behold, the day will come when all shall be carried into Babylon: nothing shall be left.'"

Micah

1. At the same time as Isaiah there lived another prophet, Micah, a countryman of Judah, who beheld with anger the wicked things that men of power and riches did to the poor.

2. "Woe to them that plan evil by night and practise it by day!" he would cry. "They take what they covet by violence, and drive out the women and children from their pleasant homes. The princes flay my people."

3. "The priest teaches for hire, the prophet divines for money; the judge can be bribed, and so Jerusalem shall be destroyed.

4. "But out of Bethlehem shall come He who is to rule Israel, whose goings forth have been from everlasting.

5. "And He shall judge and rebuke the strong nations; and they shall beat their swords into ploughshares, and spears into pruning forks. True religion is this: to do justly, to love mercy, and to walk humbly with God."

Josiah

1. During his reign of thirty-one years, Josiah, Hezekiah's grandson, ordered the high-priest, Hilkiah, to pay carpenters, builders and masons to repair the Temple.

2. During the work, Hilkiah discovered in the Temple the Book of the Law of Moses. When it was read to the King, he rent his clothes, for it condemned the idolatry——

3. —and other sins of his people. Huldah, the prophetess, foretold: "Evil will come, because the people have forsaken the Lord; but the King's eyes will not see it——

4. "—because he has humbled himself." Then Josiah and the people made a covenant with God. Idols were destroyed, and the Passover kept again.

5. But Josiah was shot at Megiddo in battle against the Egyptians, whose king, Necho, led his forces through Judah on his way to fight the Assyrians.

Jeremiah and the fall of Judah

1. In the thirteenth year of Josiah's reign God called Jeremiah, a young man of Anathoth, a village two miles from Jerusalem: "See, I have put My words in your mouth."

2. Now Necho had been defeated by the Babylonians, who put Jehoiakim on the throne of Judah. Jeremiah startled the Jews by foretelling Jerusalem's doom.

3. The Jews were angry, and when the son of the chief governor of the Temple heard what Jeremiah had prophesied, he had him beaten and put in the stocks.

4. Afterwards Jeremiah dictated to Baruch all he had prophesied, adding that the destroyer of Judah would be Babylon. Baruch read this to the people.

5. But when the roll containing the prophecies was read to King Jehoiakim, the King cut it up with his penknife, and threw it on the fire.

6. In 597 B.C., as Jeremiah had prophesied, King Nebuchadnezzar of Babylon took Jerusalem, carried off its treasures and led away many captives. Zedekiah became king.

7. Jeremiah advised the Jews remaining in the city to obey their Babylonian masters. Once again he prophesied.

8. The future, he declared, lay with the captives in Babylon; Jerusalem would be totally destroyed. His Jewish enemies accused him of undermining the people's will to resist, and cast him into a deep dungeon pit.

9. From there he was rescued by an Ethiopian of the King's household; but he remained in the court of the prison.

10. And he was still there when, eleven years later, in 586 B.C., Nebuchadnezzar destroyed the city. Many Jews fled to Egypt, forcing Jeremiah to go with them. There, tradition says, he was eventually stoned to death.

In Babylon

1. Among those captive in Babylon was a royal Jewish youth called Daniel, who was able to interpret dreams. Now King Nebuchadnezzar was troubled by a dream he could not recall.

2. His wise men could not help, but Daniel, inspired by God, told him that his dream was of an image.

3. Suddenly a stone crashed on the feet of the image, which broke, and the stone became a great mountain which filled the earth. The dream foretold the rise and fall of many kingdoms; but finally God would set up a kingdom——

4. —which would consume all kingdoms and would stand forever. And the King fell on his face before Daniel, saying: "Your God is a God of gods indeed!"

5. Then the King made Daniel a great man and a ruler in Babylon, together with Shadrach, Meshach and Abed-nego, three other young Jews of the royal house.

The burning fiery furnace

1. Nebuchadnezzar made a huge golden idol, and at its dedication proclaimed that at the sound of special music everyone must worship. But Shadrach, Meshach and Abed-nego refused.

2. Chaldean nobles informed the King of their defiance, and he angrily threatened to cast them into a furnace. "What god can save you then?" he cried.

3. "Our God is able; but even if He does not we will not worship the image," they replied. Then the strongest men in the army were ordered to bind them.

4. Fully clothed, they were flung into the burning, fiery furnace, the heat of which killed the men who did so. Suddenly the King cried: "I can see four men walking in the flames unhurt. The fourth is like the Son of God."

5. And when they came out, untouched by fire, King Nebuchadnezzar said: "Blessed be their God!"

Ezekiel's vision

1. Among those Jews first taken to Babylon was Ezekiel, a priest and a prophet. To him came visions symbolic of the doom of Jerusalem, but symbolic also of the hope of restoration.

2. In one of these visions, Ezekiel stood in a valley which was full of dry bones. "Prophesy to these bones," God told him. "Tell them that they will live, for I will give them skin and sinews and breath; and you shall know I am the Lord." Ezekiel did so. There was a noise and a shaking, and the bones came together. But they were still without life.

3. Again God spoke to Ezekiel, and the prophet obeyed Him, calling on the four winds to give to the bodies the breath of life; and they lived and stood on their feet—a great army of people. Then God said: "These bones are the whole house of Israel, and I will put My spirit into you, and bring you out of your captivity, into your own land."

241

The writing on the wall

1. When Belshazzar was King of Babylon, he gave a feast at which he and his guests praised their own idols while they drank wine from golden vessels, brought from Jerusalem by Nebuchadnezzar.

2. As they drank, the fingers of a man's hand appeared and wrote on the plaster of the wall.

3. The panic-stricken king sent for his astrologers and wise men, but they could not read the writing. Then the Queen suggested to the King that Daniel, who had "wisdom like the wisdom of the gods," should be asked to interpret it.

4. "It reads," said Daniel, "Mene, mene, tekel upharsin!" 'You are weighed in the balance and found wanting.' God has finished your kingdom, and will divide it.

5. "The Medes and Persians shall reign!" Daniel's prophecy was fulfilled; for that night Belshazzar was slain, and his kingdom was taken by Darius the Mede.

Daniel and the lions

1. King Darius honored Daniel above all other nobles in his kingdom. In their jealousy, the nobles decided to accuse Daniel through his religion, so they persuaded Darius to sign a decree.

2. By this anyone who sought a favor of any god or man, except the King, should be thrown to the lions. But Daniel continued to pray to God three times daily.

3. And so the King was forced to send Daniel to the lions' den; for it was the law of the Medes and Persians that the King's decree was unalterable.

4. In the morning, after a sleepless night thinking of Daniel, Darius hurried to the den. He called to Daniel, who replied: "My God sent an angel, and shut the lions' mouths, so I am unhurt." The King rejoiced, and ordered his men to bring Daniel out of the lions' den, and to throw his enemies to the lions in his stead.

A prophet in exile

1. Some of the greatest Hebrew prophecies, made to the Israelites in their captivity in Babylon, are to be found in the later part of the Book of Isaiah.

2. In these the Israelites were reminded that they were God's chosen people, and from among them would come God's servant, "despised and rejected by men."

3. He would bear their griefs, carry their sorrows, be wounded for their transgressions, and with His stripes heal them. The prophecy promised that the Jews would be freed from their captivity, and would return to Jerusalem, for God rules all the universe, shaping history according to His plan.

The homecoming

1. The prophet was right, for after the Jews had been for fifty years in exile King Cyrus allowed some to return, and gave back the sacred vessels taken from Solomon's Temple.

2. The first care of those captives who returned to Jerusalem was to repair the altar of burnt offering, and offer again the daily sacrifices.

3. Later they laid the foundations of a new Temple, encouraged by the high-priest, Jeshua, and the prophets Haggai and Zechariah.

4. But when the Samaritans were not allowed to help the Jews in the building, they complained to Artaxerxes, and the work had to be stopped. Later, however, Darius issued a decree, allowing the work to go on, and the new Temple was dedicated with sacrifices and great rejoicings; and priests and Levites were appointed to continue the services.

Queen Esther

1. In the days when Ahasuerus, son of Darius, was on the throne of Persia, he gave a great feast in the city of Susa for his princes and nobles. During the feast he commanded that his Queen, Vashti, should appear before them, for she was very beautiful. The King was very angry when his chamberlains told him that Vashti refused to obey.

2. He therefore decided to select another Queen in her stead. The girl he chose was Esther, the adopted daughter of a rich Jew, Mordecai. Esther did not tell the King she was a Jewess.

3. The King's life was saved by Mordecai, who overheard the plot of two of the King's officers.

246

4. Now Mordecai had an enemy, Haman, chief of the princes, for Mordecai refused to bow before him as the King commanded. In his anger Haman planned to have all the Jews in the kingdom killed.

5. He obtained the King's authority to do what he would with the Jews, and drew up an order to massacre them all. When Mordecai heard, he told Queen Esther.

6. She asked the King and Haman to a feast. The night before, the King, unable to sleep, called for his chronicles, and learned how Mordecai had saved him.

7. He called Haman, and ordered him to heap honors upon Mordecai the Jew, whom Haman hated.

8. Now Haman had built a gallows on which to hang Mordecai; but when Esther revealed his treachery against her people, Haman was hanged instead. Once again the Jews had been saved.

Nehemiah builds the walls

1. The chief cup-bearer to Artaxerxes was Nehemiah. One day he came sadly to the King.

2. When the King heard his story of the defenseless condition of Jerusalem, he gave Nehemiah permission to set out with a company to rebuild the walls of the city.

3. So Nehemiah travelled to Jerusalem with the captains of the army and horsemen. He and a few friends secretly surveyed the ruined city by night.

4. When Nehemiah urged the people of Jerusalem to rebuild the walls, the Samaritans, Sanballat the Horonite, and Tobiah the Ammonite, opposed him and conspired to fight the Jews. So the builders worked each with a weapon in his hand, and others formed a guard.

5. By an almost unbelievable effort, the work was completed and Jerusalem once again enclosed with walls and towers. At the dedication of the walls the princes of Judah and two great companies formed processions and, with rejoicing, gave their thanks to God.

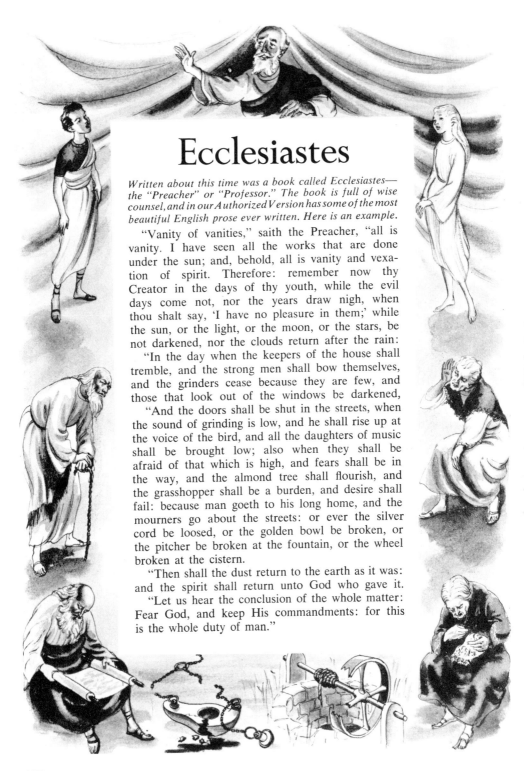

Ecclesiastes

Written about this time was a book called Ecclesiastes—the "Preacher" or "Professor." The book is full of wise counsel, and in our Authorized Version has some of the most beautiful English prose ever written. Here is an example.

"Vanity of vanities," saith the Preacher, "all is vanity. I have seen all the works that are done under the sun; and, behold, all is vanity and vexation of spirit. Therefore: remember now thy Creator in the days of thy youth, while the evil days come not, nor the years draw nigh, when thou shalt say, 'I have no pleasure in them;' while the sun, or the light, or the moon, or the stars, be not darkened, nor the clouds return after the rain:

"In the day when the keepers of the house shall tremble, and the strong men shall bow themselves, and the grinders cease because they are few, and those that look out of the windows be darkened,

"And the doors shall be shut in the streets, when the sound of grinding is low, and he shall rise up at the voice of the bird, and all the daughters of music shall be brought low; also when they shall be afraid of that which is high, and fears shall be in the way, and the almond tree shall flourish, and the grasshopper shall be a burden, and desire shall fail: because man goeth to his long home, and the mourners go about the streets: or ever the silver cord be loosed, or the golden bowl be broken, or the pitcher be broken at the fountain, or the wheel broken at the cistern.

"Then shall the dust return to the earth as it was: and the spirit shall return unto God who gave it.

"Let us hear the conclusion of the whole matter: Fear God, and keep His commandments: for this is the whole duty of man."

The trials of Job

1. The Book of Job is a dramatic poem, telling of Job, a good, God-fearing man, rich and with a large family. It was written to show that, though the good may suffer, they must keep their faith, for God knows all their sufferings and is near.

2. Satan said to God: "You have made Job secure, but let all that he has be taken away and he will curse you." "It is in your power to try him," said God.

3. And there came a day when messengers brought Job news of the loss one after another of his oxen, asses, camels, sheep and servants. While the last yet spoke——

4. —another came and cried: "Your sons and daughters were feasting in their brother's house when a wind struck it and it killed them as it fell."

5. When he heard, Job rent his cloak, shaved his head, fell upon the ground and worshipped God, saying: "The Lord gave and the Lord has taken away."

251

6. Again God gave Satan leave to try Job. And Job was covered with sore boils from head to foot.

7. "Curse God, and die," said his wife. "What!" he replied. "Shall we receive good from God and not ill?"

8. Three of Job's friends, Eliphaz, Bildad and Zophar, with a young man, Elihu, came to comfort him. For seven days they sat and spoke no word, for they saw that his sorrow was great. Then they argued that he must have done wrong and this was God's punishment.

9. But even in the midst of his grief Job found God near, and cried: "I have heard of Thee by the hearing of the ear; but now mine eye seeth Thee!"

10. So the Lord blessed the latter end of Job more than his beginning, and gave him twice as much as he had before—possessions, friends, sons and daughters.

Jonah

1. To remind the Jews of their mission to proclaim God's word to the heathen comes the story of Jonah, whom God ordered to go to Nineveh, the capital of Assyria, and to preach against the people's wickedness. But Jonah fled.

2. Hoping to escape God's will, he boarded, at Joppa, a ship bound for Tarshish. But there was a terrible storm.

3. Calling on their gods for help, the terrified sailors cast the cargo overboard, for it seemed that the ship would break in pieces.

4. Then they awoke the sleeping Jonah and decided to cast lots so that they might discover which of them had offended the gods to make them angry. The lot fell on Jonah, and he ordered the men to throw him into the sea to calm it, for he believed the storm had been created for his sake. They obeyed, and a great fish swallowed him.

5. For three days and nights, Jonah remained in the fish. Then he prayed.

6. His prayer was heard, and the fish vomited Jonah up on the shore.

7. Again God commanded Jonah to go to Nineveh. This time he obeyed, and went about the city proclaiming: "In forty days' time, Nineveh will be destroyed."

8. The King, however, heard the prophecy and proclaimed a fast for all his people. God saw their sorrow for their sins and did not destroy the city. But Jonah was angry.

9. For had he not proclaimed, as God ordered, the destruction of the city? Then he went outside the city, and built himself a little hut to watch what would happen.

10. A gourd sheltered him. He mourned when it died; and God said: "You had pity on a gourd—should I then not spare Nineveh, that great city?"

The Years Between

FOUR hundred years separate the last story told in the Old Testament, and the account of the rebuilding of the walls of Jerusalem by Nehemiah, from the first story told in the New Testament, that of the birth of Our Lord Jesus Christ.

They were four hundred years of oppression, during which the Jews clung steadfastly to their faith in God, and increasingly cherished their hope that there would come to the people a Messiah, God's Anointed One, who would set them free from the tyranny of their conquerors. In these next pages something of the story of those years is told.

RULE OF THE GREEKS

The Persian Empire of Cyrus, Darius and Artaxerxes, which had absorbed the kingdom of Judah, fell, in its turn, to the all-conquering Greek, Alexander the Great. The Jewish historian, Josephus, tells us that Alexander visited Jerusalem and worshipped in the Temple.

His rule over the Jews was a friendly one; but on his death his successors fought over the country. Ptolemy Soter, one of Alexander's generals, who had taken over Egypt, invaded Palestine, seized Jerusalem, and took captive thousands of Jews, whom he transported to Alexandria.

THE "SEPTUAGINT"

It was Ptolemy's son, Ptolemy Philadelphus, who persuaded the Jews to translate their scriptures into Greek, and so began the "Septuagint," or Old Testament in Greek, which became the Bible of the Jews outside Palestine and of the first Christians.

But another of Alexander's generals, Seleucus, had become ruler of Syria on Alexander's death; and his successors wanted Palestine for themselves. Bitter battles were fought in Palestine, and the country eventually fell into the hands of the Seleucids.

OPPOSING PARTIES

For certain sections of the Jews favored the Seleucids, and sought to save their nation not by fostering its religion but by accepting its position as an important part of the Greek Empire. They asked the support of Antiochus Epiphanes, now on the Syrian throne, and he invaded Palestine because of the disturbances created by those Jews who opposed this pro-Greek section of their people.

When he reached Jerusalem, he robbed the Temple of its sacred vessels, and even took away the veil that hid the Holy of Holies. He set a Syrian guard in a tower overlooking the Temple; and, in the Temple itself, he put

Mattathias killed the Syrian officer before the heathen altar.

up an image of the pagan god, Zeus. Then he ordered that the Jewish religion should be wiped out, and the worship of pagan idols ruthlessly enforced.

It was obvious that there would be resistance by all devout Jews to this order. The lead came from an aged priest, Mattathias, in the little town of Modin, where a heathen altar had been set up. A royal Syrian officer commanded that a sacrifice should be made to show the people's acceptance of the pagan gods. Mattathias at once killed both the officer and the Jew who had been about to perform the sacrifice.

JUDAS MACCABAEUS AND HIS BROTHERS

The loyal Jews united, and a mighty struggle developed. Mattathias died, but he left five sons to carry on his work. The first was Judas, called Maccabaeus (The Hammerer). He was victorious in many battles; and eventually won back the Temple at Jerusalem, which was cleansed and dedicated for the worship of Jehovah again. He also sent an embassy to the Roman Senate.

When at last Judas died in battle, his brother Jonathan succeeded him as the leader of the Jews and was also made high-priest. The position of the

Judas won back the Temple.

Jews was not secure, but they had become powerful enough for both the King of Syria and his rival to try to win Jonathan's support. He defeated all attempts made to conquer him, but was at last treacherously slain by Trypho, an officer of Alexander Balas, whom Jonathan had supported, and who had gained the throne of Syria.

A third brother, Simon, succeeded Jonathan, and beat off Trypho's army. Gradually, under this high-priest, the Jews won more independence, peace and prosperity, and were

allowed to coin their own money. Simon's death—he was murdered by his son-in-law—was a great disaster for the people; and so beloved was he that a brazen tablet was put in the Temple in his honor.

THE STRUGGLE CONTINUES

Simon's son, John Hyrcanus, continued the struggle of the Jews, and led them in successful wars against the Samaritans and the Edomites. Of his three sons, Aristobulus took the title "King of the Jews"; he murdered his brother Antigonus, and soon after-

The Jews coined their own money.

wards died himself, leaving his other brother, Alexander Jannaeus, to extend the power of the Jewish kingdom.

Alexander's widow, Alexandra, next ruled the country through the Pharisees, who were now powerful in the land, and her son, Hyrcanus, became high-priest. Hyrcanus and his brother, Aristobulus II, quarrelled as to who should be king, and finally it was the rich Idumean, Antipater, father of Herod the Great, who persuaded the Roman general, Pompey, to appoint Hyrcanus "King" and himself "Procurator" (Governor) of Judea.

THE ROMANS IN JERUSALEM

But when war between the adherents of the two brothers broke out, Pompey and his Roman legions themselves took a hand. Pompey laid siege to Jerusalem, and took the city. Once again, to the horror of the Jews, the Holy of Holies was entered. Thousands of Jews were massacred. Aristobulus and his family were taken captive, and Judea fell under the rule of Rome

Antipater was determined to have the support of the Romans, and when Pompey was killed in battle he at once transferred his allegiance to Caesar.

Pompey took Jerusalem and the Romans entered the Holy of Holies.

Caesar confirmed his position as Procurator, and that of Hyrcanus as high-priest.

Herod, the son of Antipater, followed his father as Procurator, and went to Rome, where he was appointed by the Senate as "King of the Jews." Then, returning to Palestine, he captured Jerusalem with Roman aid, and without mercy killed all those who opposed him.

THE REIGN OF HEROD THE GREAT

In an attempt to make friends of the Jews and so strengthen his position, Herod married Mariamne, granddaughter of Hyrcanus II, and appointed as high-priest her seventeen-year-old brother, another Aristobulus, and one of the most handsome men in Judea.

But Herod became jealous of his brother-in-law's popularity; and, it is said, when Aristobulus was bathing with other youths in the luxurious warm baths at Jericho, soldiers appeared and held him under the water until he was drowned.

Herod also murdered his wife, her two sons and another son of his. It is not surprising, therefore, that after the wise men came seeking Jesus, "He that is born King of the Jews," Herod murdered all the young children at Bethlehem.

THE TEMPLE REBUILT

But one good thing Herod the Great did for the Jews. He rebuilt the Temple with great magnificence, though only priests were allowed to do the actual building, and he himself was not allowed to set foot on the sacred soil.

As long as politics were kept separate from religion, he encouraged religion; and he managed to maintain peace throughout the country until his death.

PART III

The Story of His Church

YOU will by now have seen that the stories of the Bible are one story —the story of God seeking, through the centuries, to give men peace and goodwill on earth, and to equip them for the life of heaven.

Before He ascended, Jesus had commanded His disciples to go and preach to all nations. That they might do this work, He promised them the power of the Holy Spirit, and His own Presence—"Lo, I am with you always," He said, "even unto the end of the world."

In this section, which is based on the Acts of the Apostles and the Epistles, we shall see how the promise was fulfilled, and how the Apostles obeyed this command. We shall see them travelling abroad with their good news (Gospel) and hear of the adventures that befell them. Everywhere they went, some believed and became disciples. We shall discover the strange case of the Apostle Paul, who persecuted the Christians, but, after he met the risen Lord on the Damascus road, became the "Apostle to the Gentiles," travelling throughout the world and founding Churches wherever he went. We shall see the vision which John saw, on the Island of Patmos, of Jesus seated on His heavenly throne, and innumerable followers around Him; and the Final Judgment of all earth when God, through Jesus, will end the experiment of this Universe, "and there shall be a new heaven and a new earth."

To complete the story of the Apostles we shall turn to other early Christian writings.

In the pages entitled "The Story Continues" you will see how wonderfully and widely the Church spread before the end of the first century.

This story of the Bible is the most significant story in the history of mankind and—the story continues. Everywhere, north, south, east and west, there are those who believe that Jesus is the World's Only Hope, the Son of God and Saviour of Mankind, and whose lives are given in His service.

The story continues. You are writing it now, on the pages of history, as you think over these things and follow His guidance.

The purpose of God, of which this has been the record, is that men everywhere shall become God's sons. The coming of Jesus as Saviour and the gift of His Spirit are intended for all—for "the promise is to you and to your children, and all that are afar off, even as many as the Lord our God shall call."

The upper room

1. Returning from the Mount of Olives, where they had seen Jesus taken up in a cloud, the apostles, with other followers of Jesus, gathered in an upper room in Jerusalem, and prayed for the coming of the Holy Spirit. Peter reminded them that they must choose someone to replace Judas, who had hanged himself.

2. They must make their choice from those who had followed Jesus since His baptism. Joseph Barsabas and Matthias were put forward, and when the disciples had prayed for God's guidance, they cast lots. Matthias was chosen and numbered with the eleven.

Whitsuntide

1. Ten days after the Ascension, as they were praying, the sound of a mighty rushing wind came from Heaven, and tongues of flame rested on each of them.

2. They found that they were filled with the power of God's Spirit, and able to speak so that everyone could understand them. Jerusalem was full of people at the time, for it was the Jews' Harvest Festival, and the disciples went eagerly among them, speaking of Jesus, His work, His death and His resurrection.

3. Peter promised that if they were baptized in Jesus' name they would be freed from their sins and receive the Spirit of God. That day about three thousand were baptized, submitting to the teaching of the apostles and bringing their goods to be shared.

At the Beautiful Gate

1. Some days later Peter and John went up to the Temple at the time of prayer.

2. Lying begging at the Beautiful Gate was a man who had been a cripple from his birth, and he asked alms of Peter and John.

3. The two fixed their eyes on him. Peter said: "Look at us." Expecting money, the man did so. "I have no silver or gold——

4. "—but such as I have I give you. In the name of Jesus Christ of Nazareth, rise up and walk," said Peter. He helped up the man, who stood, then leaped and walked, praising God. When the people marvelled, Peter told them that only by faith in Jesus Christ had the man been cured.

On trial for Jesus

1. While Peter was speaking to the people, many of whom believed his message, the ruler of the Temple, with priests and Sadducees, came to arrest the apostles and imprisoned them for the night.

2. The next morning Peter and John were brought before the Sanhedrin. Annas and Caiaphas were there. The two apostles were asked: "By what power or what name have you done this?" Peter answered: "By the Name of Jesus Christ, Whom you crucified——

3. "—and Whom God raised from the dead, this man has been healed. There is salvation in no other name."

4. The Council, after a secret discussion, let the apostles go, threatening them with punishment if they taught again in Jesus' name. So they returned to the disciples and reported this. Then all joined in prayer.

Ananias and Sapphira

1. The numbers of believers grew daily. Many sold their land and houses to lay their money at the apostles' feet for sharing. One was called Barnabas.

2. Two others were Ananias and his wife Sapphira, who decided to keep some of the money, though they declared they were giving all they had received.

3. When Ananias brought the money to the apostles, Peter cried out: "Ananias, why has Satan filled your heart? You have not lied to men, but to God!"

4. At these words Ananias fell dead and was taken away to be buried. A little later Sapphira, not knowing what had happened, came in. Peter questioned her.

5. Then she, too, lied about the price of the land. Peter said: "Those who have just buried your husband are at the door." Then Sapphira also fell dead.

Gamaliel's advice

1. The Spirit of God worked so powerfully through the apostles that the sick were laid on beds in the streets, so that at least the shadow of Peter might fall on some of them.

2. Again the high-priest had the apostles arrested and put in the common prison. But at night the prison doors were opened by an angel, who commanded them to go and preach in the Temple.

3. Next day the officers found the apostles had gone. The Council heard that they were in the Temple——

4. —and again ordered the apostles before them. "Did we not command you not to teach in this Name?" asked the high-priest. "We ought to obey God rather than man," Peter replied. Then they would have killed the apostles but for the advice of Gamaliel, a leading Jewish scholar: "If it be the work of God, you cannot overthrow it."

The first martyr

1. Among the disciples were many Greek-speaking Jews. When they complained that the widows among them did not get a fair share of food in the daily distribution, seven men were chosen to look after this matter and blessed by the apostles. They were called "deacons."

2. One was Stephen, who by faith and power did miracles among the people.

3. Stephen was brought before the Council by Jews from Africa and Asia, with whom he had been in dispute, and accused of blasphemy against the Temple and the law.

4. In his defense Stephen traced God's call to the Jews throughout their history, and their persecution of the prophets. Now they had even rejected the "Just One."

5. At this they were cut to the heart, and their anger grew when Stephen said: "I see the heavens opened and the Son of Man standing on God's right hand."

6. Then with a great shout they rushed to seize him; and they threw him out of the city and stoned him even as he knelt praying: "Lord Jesus, receive my spirit: and do not blame them for this sin." With these words he died. Those stoning him laid their clothes at the feet of a young man called Saul.

Simon the sorcerer

1. Because of the persecution, many disciples left Jerusalem. Philip, another deacon, went to Samaria.

2. He taught and healed in the name of Jesus, and, seeing his miracles, many believed in his message. There was great joy in the city, and many came to be baptized. Among them was Simon, a sorcerer who made use of magic powers.

3. He was held in awe by the people in the city, but was himself impressed by Philip's miracles.

4. So that those baptized might receive the Holy Ghost, Peter came——

5. —to lay hands on them. When Simon saw the apostles' power, he offered money for their secret. "The gift of God cannot be bought," said Peter sternly. "Repent, and pray!"

Philip and the Ethiopian

1. Obeying the call of an angel of the Lord, Philip then went south towards Gaza. On the road from Jerusalem he saw, sitting in a chariot, an Ethiopian, treasurer to the Queen of Ethiopia.

2. The Ethiopian was reading the words of the prophet Isaiah, and, wanting an interpretation——

3. —he invited Philip to sit with him. He asked: "Of whom does the prophet speak when he says, 'He was led like a lamb to the slaughter'?" Then Philip told him of Jesus. As they went on their way they came to a pool.

4. The Ethiopian turned to Philip and said: "What is there to stop my being baptized?" "If you believe with your whole heart, you may be," said Philip. "I do believe that Jesus Christ is the Son of God," he replied. So Philip baptized him.

The conversion of Saul

1. Saul continued his threats of death for all disciples; and hearing that some had fled to Damascus he obtained letters to the synagogue there, authorizing him to make arrests.

2. But as he came near to Damascus there suddenly shone round him a great light from Heaven. Saul fell to the earth and heard a voice: "Saul, Saul, why do you persecute Me?" "Who art Thou, Lord?" asked the trembling Saul. "I am Jesus, Whom you are persecuting!" "Lord, what wouldst Thou have me do?" he asked.

3. The Lord answered: "Arise, and go into the city, and you will be told what you must do." When Saul got up he was blind, so his men took him by the hand and led him into the city.

4. Jesus appeared to a disciple in Damascus called Ananias and said: "Go to the house of Judas and ask for a man called Saul of Tarsus, for he has seen you in a vision——

5. "—restoring his sight. I have chosen him to bear my name to the heathen."

6. So Ananias went to the house and putting his hands on Saul said: "Brother Saul, I have been sent by Jesus, Whom you saw on the road, to restore your sight——

7. "—and so that you may be filled with the Holy Spirit." And Saul saw again and was baptized. Soon after, he began to preach in the synagogues that Jesus was God's Son.

Saul's escape from Damascus

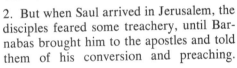

1. Night and day the Jews lay in wait at the city gates, plotting to kill Saul. So the disciples in the city let him down at night from the city walls in a basket.

2. But when Saul arrived in Jerusalem, the disciples feared some treachery, until Barnabas brought him to the apostles and told them of his conversion and preaching.

3. And every day he taught in Jerusalem in the name of Jesus, arguing with the Greek Jews that Jesus was the Messiah.

4. They also plotted to kill him. So from Caesarea he sailed to his home at Tarsus, in Cilicia, where he stayed for some years.

Miracles of Peter

1. Now Peter had been preaching up and down the country. At Lydda he found a man named Aeneas, who had been bedridden for eight years, and cured him in Jesus' name.

2. Then he went to Joppa, where there lived a disciple called Tabitha, a woman known for her kindness and work for the poor. When she fell ill, Peter was sent for.

3. But Tabitha died, and those whom she had helped wept and showed him the garments she had made for them. Peter told them to leave him alone.

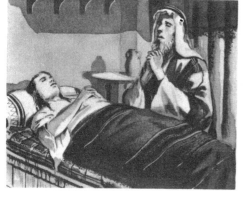

4. Then he knelt and prayed, and turning to the body of Tabitha said: "Tabitha, arise." And she opened her eyes and sat up.

5. Then Peter called the disciples and the widows whom Tabitha had helped, and showed her to them. And many believed.

Peter and Cornelius

1. In Caesarea there lived a good, devout man, Cornelius, a Roman centurion. One day an angel appeared to him in a vision, telling him to send to Joppa for Peter.

2. So he sent two servants and a soldier to the house of Simon the tanner where, the angel had said, Peter could be found.

3. Next day, as they drew near to the city, Peter went up on the roof of the house to pray; and he became hungry.

4. But while he waited for food he fell into a trance and saw let down from Heaven a great sheet in which were all sorts of animals, creeping things and birds; and a voice said: "Kill and eat." "Lord, I have never eaten food which is unclean," said Peter. "What God has made clean you should not call unclean," said God.

274

5. Even as Peter wondered about this, he heard the three men asking for him.

6. When he heard of Cornelius' vision he went to meet the Roman at his house.

7. Peter realized that God meant that he could eat with the heathen; and when Cornelius said: "We are ready to hear God's commands," he said: "I see now that God has no favorites, but accepts in every nation the man who fears Him and does good."

8. Even as Peter spoke of Jesus, the Holy Spirit filled these heathen, and they began to praise God. Then Peter ordered that they should be baptized in Jesus' name.

9. For a few days he stayed with them; then returned to Jerusalem where he told the apostles and disciples how God had called the heathen to enter the Church.

"Christians"

1. Other disciples who had been scattered at the persecution of Stephen settled in Antioch, capital of Syria. There they converted many of the Greeks to belief in Jesus.

2. When this news came to Jerusalem, Barnabas was sent to Antioch.

3. There he worked among Jesus' disciples, whose number grew daily.

4. So Barnabas went to Tarsus to bring back Saul to help in his task.

5. Because they taught that Jesus was the Christ, the Anointed King sent by God, His followers were first called Christians in Antioch.

6. When a prophet, Agabus, foretold a famine (which happened two years later), Christians in Antioch decided to send help to the Church at Jerusalem.

Peter's deliverance

1. The grandson of Herod the Great, Herod Agrippa, who was now king, began to persecute the Christians. James, the brother of John, he killed.

2. Peter he put into prison. In his cell the apostle was chained by the wrists to two soldiers, with two more on guard outside. The night before Peter was to be brought before Herod, a light shone in the prison and an angel touched him. Peter's chains fell from his hands. The angel bade him dress and follow, and Peter obeyed.

3. Peter followed the angel to the prison gates, which opened by themselves.

4. When the angel left him in the street, Peter knocked at the door of a house.

5. This house belonged to Mary, mother of John Mark, and there many of the disciples were gathered together and praying for Peter's safety.

6. A girl called Rhoda went to open the door. Hearing Peter's voice——

7. —she was so overjoyed that she ran back to the company without opening the door. They did not believe her until they had seen Peter for themselves.

8. And they were all amazed. Then he told them how the Lord had saved him; and bidding them tell the other apostles he left the country of Judea.

Saul's first missionary journey

1. It was decided in Antioch that Christians should send a mission to teach the heathen. Leaders of the Church laid hands on Saul and Barnabas, and sent them forth.

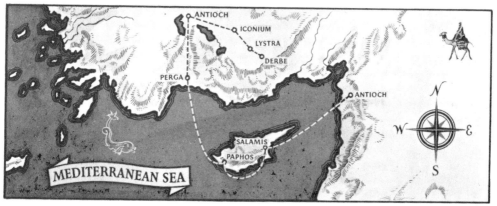

2. On this first missionary journey to establish Christian churches, Saul went by way of the island of Cyprus, to Perga and on to Antioch in Pisidia, Iconium, Lystra and Derbe. On the return journey Saul and Barnabas revisited all the cities where they had preached to strengthen the faith of the believers and returned to Antioch.

3. With them went John Mark (nephew of Barnabas) who wrote the gospel.

4. So Saul and Barnabas set out on their adventurous journey. From Antioch they travelled to Seleucia, the sea-port, and from there set sail for Cyprus.

Conversion of a Roman

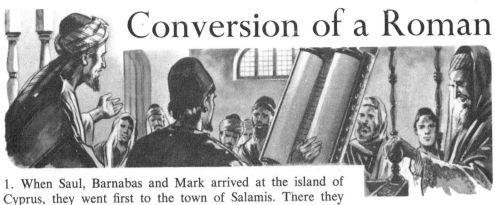

1. When Saul, Barnabas and Mark arrived at the island of Cyprus, they went first to the town of Salamis. There they preached in the synagogue on the Sabbath.

2. The Roman pro-consul, Sergius Paulus, called them to Paphos; but a false prophet, Elymas Bar-Jesus, tried to turn him away from the Faith.

3. Then Saul fixed his eyes on Elymas and denounced the sorcerer.

4. "You are a child of the devil," he cried. "And for a while you shall be blind." A mist fell on Elymas' eyes, and he begged someone to take him by the hand.

5. The pro-consul accepted the apostles' teaching and became a Christian. Then Saul, now called Paul, and the others left Paphos and continued their journey.

"We turn to the Gentiles"

1. At Perga, in Pamphylia, John Mark left to return to Jerusalem. Paul and Barnabas went on.

2. One Sabbath, in the synagogue at Antioch in Pisidia, Paul taught——

3. —that God had kept His promise to the Jews, since Jesus was the Saviour, and through Him was granted forgiveness of sins.

4. Many at once followed the apostles, but when, on the next Sabbath, the heathen also came to hear Paul, the Jews grew angry and spoke against him. He replied:

5. "Since you have spurned God's word, we turn to the heathen!" Then the Jews persuaded the leading citizens to expel Paul and Barnabas, who went on to Iconium.

281

"The gods are come down"

1. In Iconium Paul and Barnabas had to flee from hostile crowds stirred up by disbelieving Jews.

2. So they travelled to Lystra. There, as Paul preached, he saw a man listening who had been crippled since birth. "Stand upright on your feet," Paul commanded him.

3. At once the man who had never walked stood up and leaped for joy.

4. When they saw what Paul had done the people cried: "The gods are come down to us in the likeness of men!" And they called Barnabas, Jupiter, and Paul, Mercury (the messenger of the gods), because he was the chief speaker.

5. Then the priest of Jupiter's temple outside the city wall brought oxen and garlands and with the people would have sacrificed to the apostles had not Paul and Barnabas stopped them, crying: "We have come to turn you to the living God!"

6. But Jews from Antioch and Iconium came and persuaded the people to stone Paul. They dragged him from the city, thinking he was dead. But he was still alive.

7. The apostles made their way to the coast and then set sail for Antioch.

283

The Great Council

1. When certain Jewish Christians came to Antioch from Jerusalem, they insisted that all followers of Jesus ought to obey the laws which Moses laid down for the Jews. But Paul and Barnabas disagreed with their ruling in this matter.

2. So it was decided that Paul, Barnabas and other disciples should at once travel to Jerusalem to have the question settled.

3. In Jerusalem they met privately the apostles and elders of the Church, and told them of all that had been done.

4. But, as there was still opposition, the elders of the Church met in Council to discuss the matter. In the middle of the dispute Peter reminded them of God's revelation to himself that Jews and heathen should alike be saved by the grace of Jesus.

5. And it was agreed that a letter should be sent stating that it was not necessary for Christians to be bound by Moses' law.

6. The letter was brought to Antioch by Paul and Barnabas and two other disciples, one of whom, Silas, decided to stay.

Paul's second missionary journey

1. Paul's second missionary journey carried him into Europe. He and Silas went overland into Galatia, visiting the churches he had established on the earlier journey; on to Troas; thence to Philippi, Thessalonica, Athens and Corinth; sailed from Cenchrea to Ephesus, and from there back to Palestine.

2. Paul had suggested, after the Council, that he and Barnabas should visit again the Christians in all cities where they had preached. Barnabas was willing, but Paul could not agree with him to take John Mark, who had left them at Perga on their first journey.

3. So they parted. Paul, with Silas as his companion, went through Syria and Cilicia.

4. Timothy, a disciple since Paul's former visit, joined them at Derbe.

5. Paul, Silas and Timothy went on together through Phrygia and Galatia. Paul was anxious to go into Bithynia to preach, but the Holy Spirit held him back.

6. And instead they went westwards to Troas, in Mysia, and there met Luke, a doctor from Macedonia who became Paul's companion in his future travels.

7. That night Paul had a vision in which he saw a man of Macedonia, who said: "Come over and help us." Next day Paul and his friends sailed for Samothrace and Neapolis, thus crossing into Europe. They went on to Philippi.

Into Europe

1. At Philippi Paul baptized a rich woman, Lydia, and her household; and she begged Paul and his companions to stay at her house.

2. A young girl, possessed by spirits, who earned money for her masters by fortune-telling, kept shouting after Paul and Luke:

3. "These men are servants of God and show us His way of salvation!" But Paul, in Jesus' name, healed her madness.

4. When her masters saw that the source of their gain had gone, they caught Paul and Silas and dragged them off to the court——

5. —and accused them of teaching customs unlawful for the Romans. The magistrates had them beaten and put in the stocks.

6. At midnight, while Paul and Silas sang praises to God, an earthquake opened the prison doors——

7. —and loosed the prisoners' chains. The jailer, fearing all had escaped, took his sword.

8. He was about to kill himself when Paul cried: "We are all here!" He ran in. "What must I do to be saved?" he asked.

9. "Believe in Jesus," they replied. The jailer took them to his home and washed their stripes. His family was baptized.

10. Next day, when the order for their release came, Paul refused to leave the prison unless the magistrates fetched them.

11. "We are Roman citizens, imprisoned without trial!" he said. The magistrates begged them to go. So they went.

"The unknown god"

1. At Thessalonica, Paul, for three Sabbaths, taught that Jesus was the Messiah, and won many followers. But some of the Jews aroused the rabble who attacked the house where Paul was staying. Not finding him there, they dragged others of the brethren to court, charging them with saying that Jesus, not Caesar, was king.

2. They were released on a pledge to keep the peace. That night Paul and Silas set off.

3. At Berea they parted, Paul going on alone to Athens. There he reasoned again with the Jews in the synagogue, and daily in the market-place with the Greeks.

4. They were interested in any new philosophy, and led Paul to Mars' Hill to hear him. There he told of how he had seen an altar inscribed: "To the unknown god." "Him," said Paul, "I will make plain to you through Jesus, Whom He raised from the dead."

Tent-makers

1. From Athens, Paul went on to Corinth, a seaport rich, luxurious and full of evil. There he lived and worked at his old trade of tent-making with Aquila and Priscilla, Jews who had left Italy because the Emperor Claudius had expelled all Jews from Rome. Silas and Timothy joined him.

2. In the synagogue every Sabbath he tried to convince the Jews, but they opposed and blasphemed him until at last he said: "Henceforth I go to the heathen!"

3. So Paul went to live with Justus, a heathen whose house adjoined the synagogue.

4. But Crispus, a ruler of the synagogue, believed; and was baptized with his family.

5. Paul lived there for a year and a half. Then the Jews accused him of unlawful religious preaching. But Gallio, the Roman pro-consul, dismissed them.

Paul's third missionary journey

1. Paul sailed from Corinth with Aquila and Priscilla, whom he left at Ephesus, promising to return later. He went on to Caesarea, reported to the Church at Jerusalem all that had happened, and returned to Antioch.

2. Paul now began his third missionary journey, visiting again those parts of Asia and Europe where the Church had been established. Now, his friends at Ephesus——

3. —had been impressed by the powerful preaching of Apollos, a Jew from Alexandria. Although he had received only John's baptism, he preached Jesus as the Christ.

4. Aquila and Priscilla taught him further, and sent him to Corinth, where he helped to sustain the faith of the Christians.

5. Paul also, when he reached Ephesus, baptized, in Jesus' name, twelve disciples of John, and they received the Holy Spirit.

6. For two years Paul remained in Ephesus, teaching and preaching and sending the word of God through Asia. In addition, he performed many miracles of healing in the name of Jesus.

7. Even towels or aprons belonging to him were taken and used to restore the sick and suffering.

8. Ephesus was full of people who used witchcraft. Seven vagabond Jews attempted to copy Paul, and to heal a madman in the name of Jesus.

9. But the madman cried: "Jesus I know, and Paul I know—but who are you?" And he leaped up on them in a frenzied attack, so that they fled.

10. When this became known many people publicly burned their magic books.

11. In Ephesus many silversmiths lived by selling images of the goddess, Diana. One, Demetrius, stirred up the workers, saying: "Men, our craft is in danger!

12. "This Paul," he went on, "not only sets the people against our images, but against even the temple and worship of Diana!" Now Ephesus was the centre of the cult of this Asiatic goddess, and under her protection. The angry silversmiths rushed into the streets, shouting:

13. "Great is Diana of the Ephesians!" A riot developed, and two of Paul's companions were carried off by the mob.

14. They were taken to the public theatre. Paul was anxious to speak to the crowd, but his disciples held him back.

15. There was uproar in the theatre for some time. At length the town clerk addressed them: "We shall find ourselves in trouble about today's riot, for these men have neither robbed Diana's temples, nor blasphemed against her. If Demetrius is right, let him go to the law!"

Trouble at Corinth

1. Shortly afterwards, Paul left for Macedonia. But while he was at Ephesus, news had been brought by Apollos of trouble among the Christians at Corinth. Paul wrote them a letter, warning them not to mix with evil people; and he sent Timothy——

2. —to add weight to his advice. But reports of fresh strife reached him.

3. He heard of quarrels and evil living. "Remember only Jesus Christ," Paul wrote.

4. The news became worse, so Paul hurried across the sea to Corinth himself.

5. But they refused to hear him. In sorrow he returned to Ephesus, wrote a severe letter warning them he would return.

6. Paul was in Macedonia when Titus brought news that the Corinthians had repented. So Paul went to Corinth.

295

Farewells and warnings

1. Paul had planned to go direct from Corinth to Palestine, with gifts for the poor of Jerusalem.

2. But to escape a Jewish plot he was forced to go back through Macedonia, then sail to Troas, where he met the others. They stayed for seven days.

3. On his last day there, a Sunday, Paul preached to the disciples until midnight. Eutychus, a young man, fell asleep in the window-seat.

4. As he slept he fell from the window, three storeys up, into the street. Paul ran down and, taking Eutychus in his arms, brought him back to life.

5. At Miletus, Paul summoned the elders of the Ephesian Church, who wept when he said: "You will not see my face again. Trouble and danger await me. Farewell: take care of the flock, for after I have gone, wolves will enter in among you."

6. At Caesarea, Paul and his friends stayed with Philip. One day Agabus, the prophet, visited them. He bound his own hands and feet with the Apostle's girdle, saying: "Thus will the Jews bind you and deliver you to the Gentiles." "I am ready not only to be bound but to die for the Lord Jesus," Paul replied.

7. Then, in spite of his friends' pleas to stay away from Jerusalem, Paul completed his journey to that city, where he was greeted by James, the brother of Jesus, and all the elders of the Church. Paul told them of all the work that had been done among the heathen in God's name.

297

Paul's arrest

1. Now it was the Feast of Pentecost, and some of the pilgrims in the city were from Ephesus. They, recognizing Paul in the Temple, inflamed the Jews by declaring: "This is the man who set everyone against our people and our Law!" Paul was dragged out of the Temple by the mob and was beaten.

2. He was about to be killed when news that the whole of Jerusalem was in an uproar was brought to the captain of the Roman guard.

3. The captain, with a band of soldiers, ran to the scene of the riot, rescued Paul and at once arrested him, binding him with chains.

4. Paul was carried off by the soldiers to save him from the violence of the crowd. On the steps leading to the castle he was allowed to speak to the mob. He told them how Jesus had appeared to him and commanded him to preach to the heathen. "Away with him!" they shouted, when he had finished. "He is not fit to live!"

5. It was ordered that Paul should be scourged. But Paul said to the centurion in charge: "Is it lawful to scourge a Roman citizen uncondemned?"

6. The centurion warned the captain that Paul was a Roman. "Is this true?" asked the captain. "Yes," Paul replied. "I was free born." At this, the captain was afraid.

Paul before the Sanhedrin

1. Paul was at once unbound. Next morning he appeared before the Sanhedrin, summoned to explain the uproar. Realizing that some were Pharisees and some Sadducees, Paul cried: "I am a Pharisee, son of a Pharisee, yet my belief in resurrection is being questioned!"

2. For Paul knew that the Pharisees believed that the faithful survived bodily death, while the Sadducees did not. Fierce dissension at once arose among them.

3. Fearing that Paul would be torn to pieces by them, the Roman captain removed him to the barracks. There Jesus appeared to him. "Be of good cheer, Paul," He said.

4. A plot by a band of forty Jews to kill Paul when he next appeared before the Sanhedrin was overheard by Paul's nephew.

5. Paul sent him to the captain. At once Paul was removed to Caesarea to be tried by the Roman governor, Felix.

Paul and Felix

1. When, after five days, Paul's accusers arrived from Jerusalem, Felix heard the case against him.

2. Tertullus, the spokesman for the Jews, declared that Paul had stirred up trouble everywhere; that he was a ringleader of the Nazarene sect, and had profaned the Temple. Paul denied all this in his defense. "They really accuse me because I believe Jesus rose from the dead," he told Felix. Felix refused to make a decision on this evidence.

3. "I must hear more from Lysias, the captain," he said. He ordered that Paul should be guarded by a centurion.

4. But he was allowed to see his friends. Both Felix and his Jewish wife, Drusilla, visited him to hear about Jesus.

"I appeal to Caesar!"

1. Two years later, a new governor, Festus, replaced Felix. The Jews insisted on a new trial, and demanded that it should be held in Jerusalem. "I appeal to Caesar!" Paul cried.

2. "To the Emperor you shall go," said Festus, knowing that Paul, as a Roman citizen, was within his rights.

3. But when King Agrippa, the last of the Herods, came with Bernice, his sister, to pay his respects to the Roman governor, Festus asked his advice about Paul. The next day Agrippa sat with Festus to hear Paul.

4. Festus explained that he had found in Paul no crime punishable by death, for which the Jews called. Then Agrippa commanded Paul to speak. Paul told how he met the risen Lord on the Damascus road. "I was not disobedient to the heavenly vision," he continued, "but have taught both Jews and heathens that they should repent and turn to God."

5. Festus called out: "Paul, too much learning has made you mad!"

6. "I am not mad," Paul replied quietly, "but am speaking the sober truth."

7. Then he turned to King Agrippa. "I speak openly of these things before the King because I am convinced that he must already know everything that has happened. Nothing has been hidden from him, or done in a hole-and-corner way. King Agrippa, do you believe the prophets? I know that you do!" Agrippa answered wryly:

8. "You almost persuade me to become a Christian!" Paul cried: "I would to God that not only you, but all who hear me this day——

9. "—were altogether as I am!" Later they agreed amongst themselves that, had Paul not appealed to Caesar, he might have been freed.

Sailing for Rome

1. Some weeks later Paul, with other prisoners and Luke and Aristarchus, in the charge of a centurion from Rome called Julius, set sail from the harbor of Caesarea.

2. When they reached Myra, in Lycia, they boarded a grain ship, bound for Italy. Their first call was Fair Havens, a harbor in the island of Crete.

3. The journey to Fair Havens had been difficult; and Paul warned the centurion that it was dangerous to the ship, the cargo and themselves to sail on.

4. But in spite of the warning and the October gales, the centurion trusted the judgment of the ship's captain that they should make for a larger harbor.

5. They set off in a fair wind, but a hurricane swiftly blew up and the ship was driven before the wind. With great difficulty, they hauled in the ship's boat.

6. Then they undergirded the ship with cables, and struck sail, for fear they would be driven on to the sandbanks. Next day, terribly battered by the storm, they began to throw the cargo overboard. "On the third day we threw the ship's tackle overboard," wrote Luke.

7. For many days neither sun nor stars could be seen, and all hope that they could possibly be saved was abandoned. But then Paul spoke cheeringly to them.

8. "Not one of you shall lose your lives, even if the ship is lost," he said, "for an angel told me last night that I shall indeed be brought before Caesar.

9. "But we shall be wrecked on a certain island." And on the fourteenth night the crew took soundings and found that they were running into shallower water.

10. Then they feared that the ship might run on to the rocks, so they put down four anchors to hold her and waited impatiently for the dawn.

11. Now some of the crew had tried to escape in the ship's boat; but Paul warned Julius that unless every one of them remained in the ship, none would be saved.

12. So the soldiers cut the ropes of the boat, and cast it off. Then Paul urged them all to eat, and said grace; and he repeated his promise of safety.

13. At daybreak they sighted unknown land, and decided to run aground in a creek. The stern of the ship began to break up. The soldiers wanted to kill the prisoners.

14. They feared that some of them might swim out and escape. Julius was able to protect the prisoners, being anxious to save Paul. He gave orders that those who could swim should first jump into the sea and make for the land, while the rest should make their way on pieces of board and broken pieces of the ship.

Paul at Malta

1. The centurion's orders were obeyed, and, as Paul had promised, they all escaped from the wreck, not one life being lost. The land they had seen was the shore of an island whose name, they discovered, was Malta. The inhabitants showed them great kindness and welcomed them all, lighting fires for them because of the rain and cold.

2. Paul himself gathered a bundle of sticks and laid it on the fire; and a viper came out of the heat and fastened to his hand. The islanders expected to see him die.

3. Vengeance, they thought, had caught up with a murderer, even though he was saved from the sea. But Paul was unharmed —and then they said he must be a god!

4. In the same part of the island were the estates of the island's governor, a man called Publius. Hospitably he opened his doors to those who had been shipwrecked, and lodged them for three days, showing great courtesy.

5. Now the father of Publius lay ill with fever and dysentery. Paul prayed and laid hands on him—and he was cured.

6. When the islanders heard of this many of them that were ill or diseased came to the Apostle and were healed by him.

7. They held Paul and his companions in great honor, and when, three months later, the party left, loaded them with gifts. They embarked in a ship, the *Castor and Pollux,* calling at the island on its way from Alexandria, stayed at Syracuse in Sicily for three days, and then, a south wind blowing, sailed on to Rhegium, in Italy.

Paul reaches Rome

1. After only a day at Rhegium, the ship moved on to Puteoli, on the west coast. There Paul and his companions found several disciples with whom they stayed for a week. Then they went on towards Rome.

2. Many of the Roman Christians met them at Appii Forum, forty miles from the city, and at "The Three Taverns."

3. When they reached Rome, Paul was not handed over with the other prisoners but was allowed to live alone under guard.

4. After three days in Rome, Paul summoned the elders of the Jews to explain his position to them. They were quite willing to hear him, and he spoke earnestly to them, explaining to them how the life and death of Jesus was the fulfilment of the Law and the Prophets. Many believed; but they could not all agree.

Paul's death in Rome

1. Paul lived in his house in Rome for two years. The Church grew rapidly in the city, and he was allowed to receive disciples to teach them and preach to them. Some of the Emperor Nero's own household became Christians. Among his old companions were Luke, Aristarchus, Aquila and Priscilla, Timothy and Titus.

2. Titus was appointed the first head of the Christian Church at Crete, where Paul had stayed on his way to Rome.

3. And Timothy, who had been a disciple since Paul's first missionary journey, became leader of the Church at Ephesus.

4. It was from Rome, while awaiting trial before the Emperor Nero, that Paul wrote his "epistle to the Philippians," to Philemon, about his runaway slave, Onesimus, to "the Ephesians" and to "the Colossians."

5. When he knew that he was to suffer death, Paul wrote to Timothy at Ephesus: "I am ready to be offered up. The time of my departure is at hand. Come quickly to me before winter, and bring Mark with you." He gave news of some of his former companions, adding: "Only Luke is with me."

6. Paul probably met his death in A.D. 64, being beheaded on the Ostian Way, outside Rome. He had written to Timothy: "I have fought a good fight, I have finished my course, I have kept the faith; there is laid up for me a crown of righteousness."

The Revelation of St. John

In the last years of the first century, John saw a vision of Jesus, "the Lamb of God slai
for us all," sitting on the throne of the universe surrounded by "ten thousand times te
thousand, and thousands of thousands." Again, he saw Him standing on the hill wher
Jerusalem lay—Mount Sion—and the gospel being preached to every nation. Once mor
Jesus sat on a great white throne; and John saw the final judgment of the earth

The dead, both great and small, stood before God; the book of life was opened, and the dead were judged according to their works, which were written in the book. Then death and hell, and all things evil, were cast into a lake of fire; and there was a new heaven and a new earth. Those from among all nations who had believed in Jesus and followed Him on earth walked about in glorious light in an eternal city, the New Jerusalem.

The Story Continues

WHAT a wonderful picture this Story of the Bible has given to us. It has spanned the ages from God's creation of the universe, through the long years of His dealings with Israel, to the coming of His Son and the first beginnings of the Christian Church. Now we have travelled as far as the Bible itself takes us. But it is not the end of the story. The establishment of the Church is the beginning of a new chapter in the annals of God's work among men. Jesus had said to His disciples: "All power is given unto Me in heaven and on earth. Go therefore, and teach all nations, baptizing them in the name of the Father and of the Son and of the Holy Spirit; teaching them to observe all that I have commanded you; and lo, I am with you always, even to the end of the world." He had also promised them: "You shall receive power after the Holy Spirit has come upon you; and you shall be witnesses to Me both in Jerusalem, and in all Judea, and in Samaria, and unto the uttermost part of the earth." Always, as His disciples obeyed His command, they received the fulfilment of His promise.

For the rest of the story of the apostles we must turn to ancient writings and traditions.

PAUL AND HIS COMPANIONS

Paul, as we have already seen, at the end of the Acts of the Apostles, was a prisoner in Rome.

It seems probable that at the end of two years he was released, and fulfilled the ambition he had mentioned in his letter to the Romans, of going westwards to Spain. Clement of Rome, writing towards the end of the first century, tells of his "reaching the farthest bounds of the West"; and another old document, called the Muratorian Fragment, mentions expressly Spain.

Peter was sentenced to death by the Roman Emperor Nero.

314

Then, it seems, he turned again to the East, revisiting Crete, where he left Titus in charge of the Church, with the responsibility of directing and expanding the Christian work there. From Crete he most probably went to Ephesus and appointed Timothy, whom he had taken as his companion on his third missionary journey, to lead the Ephesian Christians; then inland to Colossae to stay with Philemon. It would seem from his letters to Timothy that he visited Corinth, Macedonia, Miletus and Troas, and intended to spend the winter at Nicopolis, in Thrace. But he was arrested on some charge brought by Alexander, the coppersmith of Ephesus, and hurried back to Rome.

PERSECUTION OF THE CHRISTIANS

There, the Christian Church had grown rapidly; but when, in A.D. 64, a large part of Rome was burned down, the Christians had been accused of setting fire to the city and were being violently persecuted. The Emperor Nero ordered their arrest, imprisonment and death. They suffered terribly for their Faith—many were hung as living torches in the Emperor's gardens, or thrown to the lions in the Colosseum. Paul may have arrived again in Rome during this period of persecution, was tried and condemned to death. Being a Roman citizen, he was doubtless beheaded. Tradition places the site of his execution at Tre Fontane on the Ostian Way, three miles outside the city, and points to the year A.D. 64-5.

Many Christians were thrown to the lions.

PETER'S DEATH

Peter, meanwhile, had apparently been founding churches in North and Central Asia; but there is some reason to think that he came to Rome and was arrested and sentenced to death by Nero—probably in the same year as Paul. There is a legend that when Peter was condemned to be crucified, he cried that he was not worthy to die in the same manner as his Lord, and so was hung on a cross upside down.

Papias, Bishop of Hierapolis, writing in the early part of the second century, tells us that before his death Peter told John Mark everything that he remembered about Jesus.

We know from the Acts of the Apostles that James the brother of John had been killed "with the sword" by Herod Agrippa I.

"THE UTTERMOST PART"

The rest of the apostles travelled far to bring the message of Jesus Christ to the world. Thomas, it is said, went to Parthia (Persia) and tradition says

he reached India. Bartholomew, too, it has been said, went as far as India, having preached the gospel in Arabia. Matthew is alleged to have established himself in Ethiopia — the modern Abyssinia; while Andrew, according to tradition, preached in Scythia (the south-east of modern Europe, between the Carpathians and the Caucasus, Thrace and Asia Minor). He is said to have been crucified at Patras, in Achaea.

It is said that Thomas reached India.

The Church historian, Eusebius, quotes a tradition that Thaddeus, shortly after the Ascension of Jesus, went to Edessa in North-west Mesopotamia, where he converted the king, Abgarus, to Christianity. Eusebius also records a legend that Abgarus had, some years before, sent a message to Jesus, asking Him to come and heal his disease; and that Jesus had replied that He would send one of His disciples after His Ascension.

JAMES "THE JUST"

Of the other disciples, James, the brother of Jesus, became leader of the Christians in Jerusalem. Paul, in his Epistles to the Galatians, spoke of James, Peter and John as being "the pillars" of the Church. James is said to have been so continually on his knees in the Temple that "they became as hard as a camel's." Even the Jews were filled with awe at his devotion and holiness, and named him "the Just." But during the celebrations of a Feast of the Passover, when Jewish feeling against the Christians ran high, he was thrown down from a tower of the Temple, stoned and clubbed to death.

MARK'S WORK

John Mark, who, as we have seen, was companion to both Peter and Paul, is said to have founded and presided over the Church at Alexandria, in Egypt, and to have written the "Gospel according to St. Mark." "Mark," says Papias, "having become the interpreter of Peter, wrote down accurately everything that he remembered. Mark made no mistake, for he made it his one care not to omit anything that he heard, or to set down any false statement therein."

James was continually on his knees.

316

John used to say over and over again: "Little children, love one another."

JOHN THE APOSTLE

Of the Apostle John many lovely legends are told. It is said that on one occasion, when visiting a church, he won over for Christ a youth whom he commended for special care and training. Some years later he returned to the same place, and found that the man had become a robber chieftain. Hearing this, John called for a horse, and himself rode off into the mountains to find him. There he begged him to return and repent. The bandit wept when he saw the beloved Apostle, and went back with him to the church where he had become a Christian. Nor would the Apostle leave him until he was fully restored.

John is reported to have taken charge of the churches in Asia, and to have

been arrested during the persecution of the Christians under the Emperor Domitian. One legend says that at first he was condemned to death and thrown into a cauldron of boiling oil, but by a miracle was saved, only to be exiled to the island of Patmos, in the Aegean. On his release he settled at Ephesus.

"LOVE ONE ANOTHER"

He lived to a great age; and when he was very old, tradition says, and unable any longer to preach to the people, he used to be carried into the church and repeat over and over again the words: "Little children, love one another." When he was asked why he so often repeated the words, he replied: "If this one thing were attained, it would be enough."

INDEX

319

THE BIBLE

IN PICTURES

In memory of Jesus Christ

who was born into this World as a little child and later gave His life on the Cross so that all who believe in Him may be saved

This Bible is Presented

To

Lucy Petrucelli

By

Lenten Award 1961

This Special Edition Prepared for

and

Through the Courtesy

of

The Harding Foundation • Raymondville, Texas